TOP **10**
ISRAEL
INCLUDING SINAI & PETRA

VANESSA BETTS

D0858672

EYEWITNESS TRAVEL

Contents

Left **Praying at the Western Wall** Center **Altar, Church of the Holy Sepulchre** Right **Hebron glass**

LONDON, NEW YORK,
MELBOURNE, MUNICH AND DELHI
www.dk.com

Printed and bound in China by
South China Printing Co. Ltd.

First American Edition, 2012

12 13 14 15 10 9 8 7 6 5 4 3 2 1

**Copyright 2012 © Dorling
Kindersley Limited, London
A Penguin Company**

Published in Great Britain
by Dorling Kindersley Limited

ISSN 1479-344X
ISBN 978 0 7566 9164 6

A catalog record for this book is available from
the Library of Congress.

Within each Top 10 list in this book, no
hierarchy of quality or popularity is implied. All
10 are, in the editor's opinion, of roughly equal
merit.

MIX
Paper from
responsible sources
FSC
www.fsc.org   FSC™ C018179

Contents

Israel, Sinai & Petra's Top 10

Left **Basilica of the Agony** Center **Hummus** Right **Old Jaffa port**

Left **Christ's Tomb** Right **Children at Jerusalem Biblical Zoo**

Key to abbreviations
Adm *admission charge*

ISRAEL, SINAI & PETRA'S TOP 10

ISRAEL, SINAI & PETRA'S TOP 10

TOP 10 Israel, Sinai & Petra's Highlights

This tiny strip of land is holy to the world's three great monotheistic religions, with a corresponding wealth of history, monuments, ruins, and places of worship to discover. The region also offers extraordinary natural beauty and amazing contrasts, from the forested slopes of the Galilee, to Mediterranean white-sand beaches and the harsh desert vistas of the Negev, Petra, and Sinai. Although politics here will remain contentious, travel throughout the region is remarkably safe and secure, meaning pilgrims and travelers continue to come as they have since antiquity.

1 Church of the Holy Sepulchre
The holiest church in the world is built over the site where, tradition says, Jesus was crucified on the cross. Even amid the spiritual frenzy, it is possible to touch the rock of Golgotha and to enter Christ's Tomb (see pp8–9).

Haram esh-Sharif (Temple Mount) 2
Meaning "Noble Sanctuary," Haram esh-Sharif is a huge platform topped by the spectacular gold-leaf and mosaic covered Dome of the Rock – the quintessential image of Jerusalem (see pp10–11).

3 The Citadel (Tower of David)
Greeting visitors who enter the Old City through Jaffa Gate, this fortification has survived for more than 20 centuries, destroyed and rebuilt by invaders from the Crusaders to the Ottomans (see pp12–13).

4 Israel Museum
The renovated Israel Museum houses an encyclopedic collection of art, archaeology, and Jewish artifacts, plus the iconic Shrine of the Book displaying the Dead Sea Scrolls (see pp14–17).

5 The Mount of Olives
Although no longer covered with olive trees, this hill bestows a stunning aspect of Jerusalem. Adorned with churches, the Mount of Olives holds a crucial place in Jewish and Christian tradition (see pp18–19).

Preceding pages **Western Wall plaza**

Bethlehem 6

As Jesus's birthplace, Bethlehem has been a major pilgrimage center since the 4th century. Yet the town remains unchanged, and its square, market, and streets retain an authentic air *(see pp20–21)*.

Jaffa 7

The fortunes of this port have waxed and waned through the ages, but today Old Jaffa boasts a wealth of renovated Ottoman architecture and brims with art galleries, cultural centers, restaurants, and varied shopping options *(see pp22–3)*.

Masada 8

Perched atop a mountain plateau, this fortress is a formidable sight. In the 1st century AD, around 1,000 Jewish rebels chose suicide over surrender to Roman rule here. The plateau is on the edge of the Dead Sea, adding to Masada's mystique *(see pp24–5)*.

St. Catherine's Monastery 9

Nestled at the foot of Mount Sinai, this monastery is reputed to be site of the Burning Bush and contains the relics of St. Catherine. Precious icons and manuscripts are displayed in a museum here *(see pp26–7)*.

Petra – The Siq 10

The entrance to Petra is lined with sacred niches carved with ancient graffiti, and paved with a road that is 2,000 years old. This cleft in the rock creates an atmosphere of anticipation that is enhanced by the first glimpse of the Treasury at its far end *(see pp28–9)*.

TOP 10 Church of the Holy Sepulchre

Venerated as the site of the crucifixion and resurrection of Jesus, this is the holiest venue in all Christendom, and an intensely spiritual place – irrespective of one's religious persuasion. In AD 326, Emperor Constantine began building the first church here. The basilica was destroyed by the Persians in AD 614 and by the Fatimid Sultan Hakim in 1009, then rebuilt by the Crusaders between 1114 and 1170. The church survived a fire in 1808 and an earthquake in 1927, so today, it represents a mix of historical periods and restorations.

Courtyard, Church of the Holy Sepulchre

🕐 There is only one entrance door, via the courtyard, into the Church. Wheelchair users will not be able to enter Christ's Tomb, Golgotha, or the side chapels, but can safely negotiate the main area of the Church.

🍴 There are several restaurants and cafes at the Muristan *(see p58)*, only a minute's walk from the Church's entrance.

- Map P4
- The Christian Quarter
- (02) 626 7000
- Light Rail to City Hall, or Egged bus 60 to Jaffa Gate
- Open 4am–7pm daily; summer: 5am–9pm

Top 10 Features

1 Courtyard
2 Stone of Unction
3 Golgotha
4 Chapel of Adam
5 The Rotunda
6 Chapel of St. Helena
7 Ethiopian Monastery
8 Christ's Tomb
9 Catholikon Dome
10 Syrian Chapel

Courtyard

The courtyard, known as the Parvis, is lined with tiny chapels belonging to various denominations. The imposing facade of the Church is Crusader, with marble pillars flanking the doors and fine stonework on the upper levels.

Stone of Unction

This stone marks the spot where Christ's body was anointed and wrapped before burial. The stone dating from the 12th century was destroyed in the fire of 1808. A smooth limestone slab installed in 1810 marks its location *(above)*.

Golgotha

Well-worn steps lead to the Rock of Golgotha, which commemorates the site of the crucifixion with glorious altars and glinting mosaics. Beneath the Greek Orthodox altar *(main image)*, it's possible to touch the rock itself.

Chapel of Adam

The lower section of the Rock of Golgotha can be seen here. The fissure in the rock is believed to have been caused by the earthquake after the crucifixion *(above)*.

The Rotunda
A dome decorated with a 12-pointed star rises above the Rotunda *(above)*. The colonnade was rebuilt after 1808 but two pillars still remain from the original basilica.

Chapel of St. Helena
This chapel, under Armenian custodianship, dates back to Crusader times. The walls of the steps leading down to it are marked with crosses carved by early pilgrims.

Ethiopian Monastery
These cells on the roof of the Chapel of St. Helena have been occupied by the Ethiopians since the 17th century *(above)*. A door leads down to the Ethiopian chapel, through a Coptic Chapel, and then down to the Parvis.

ΞΕΝΩΘΕΝΤΙ ΔΕΣΠΟΤΑ ΧΡΙΣΕ.

Christ's Tomb
At the heart of the Church, and the focal point for devotees, is this marble shrine built around the place where Christ's body was supposedly laid *(right)*. The current shrine dates from 1809–10 and comprises two chapels.

Catholikon Dome
Decorated with an image of Christ, the Catholikon Dome *(right)* covers the central nave of the Crusader church. The omphalos, a stone basin beneath the dome, reflects the medieval belief that this was the center of the world.

Syrian Chapel
Accessed through the rear wall of the Rotunda, this dilapidated chapel contains Jewish rock-cut tombs dating from 100 BC–AD 100. The candlelit tombs give an impression of how Christ's burial place would originally have looked.

The Holy Fire
In the Greek Orthodox faith Holy Saturday is when the Miracle of the Holy Fire symbolizes the resurrection of Christ. The Greek Orthodox Patriarch leads the ceremony, which sees an unlit candle burst into flame inside Christ's Tomb. This heaven-lit candle is then used to light the candles of worshippers, who gather to witness the miracle. Holy Fire falls on May 4th in 2013.

Haram esh-Sharif (Temple Mount)

The focal point of Jerusalem, the traditional site of Solomon's First Temple, an important Islamic religious sanctuary – the Haram esh-Sharif is probably the most contentious piece of land on Earth. Herod the Great built the Second Temple here, but his colossal complex was razed by the Romans in AD 70, and the site was left derelict until the arrival of Islam in the 7th century. The iconic Dome of the Rock stands at the center today, while all that remains of Herod's temple is a section of the outer retaining wall, revered by Jews as the Western Wall.

Minbar of Burhan al-Din

🌀 Entry to the Haram esh-Sharif is restricted to a few hours Sunday through Thursday. Non-Muslims can enter only through the Moors' Gate (Bab el-Maghariba) via a covered wooden ramp, but can exit through any of the operational gates. Non-Muslims cannot enter the Dome of the Rock or El-Aqsa Mosque.

🍽 Try the Old City's best hummus at Abu Shukri on Al-Wad St. *(see p43)*, but note that it can get quite crowded during lunchtime.

• Map Q4 • Entrance via Moors' Gate, next to the Western Wall Plaza
• (02) 622 6250
• Egged buses 1 and 3 to the Western Wall
• Open summer: 7:30–11am & 1:30–2:30pm Sun–Thu; winter: 7:30–10am & 12:30–1.30pm Sun–Thu

Top 10 Features

1. Dome of the Rock
2. El-Aqsa Mosque
3. Solomon's Stables
4. Dome of the Chain
5. Golden Gate
6. Ashrafiyya Madrasa
7. El-Kas Fountain
8. Minbar of Burhan al-Din
9. Qanatir
10. Sabil of Qaitbey

Dome of the Rock
Built in AD 688–91 by Caliph Abd el-Malik, this shrine is one of the world's great architectural glories. A synthesis of Byzantine and Classical styles, the octagonal building *(main image)* was constructed with mathematical precision to enshrine the Holy Rock within.

El-Aqsa Mosque
Built in the early 8th century, El-Aqsa *(above)* was razed by earthquakes and occupied by the Crusaders. The interior has a *mihrab* (prayer niche) from Saladin's time and marble columns donated by Mussolini.

Solomon's Stables
This structure is part of the underground vaulting system *(below)* built by Herod to support the Haram esh-Sharif. It became a mosque in 1996, and can accommodate 10,000 worshippers.

4 Dome of the Chain
Supported by 17 columns, the Dome of the Chain's purpose remains a mystery. The 13th-century tiling on the dome's interior is as exquisite as that inside the Dome of the Rock.

5 Golden Gate
Jewish tradition states that the Messiah will enter Jerusalem through this Herodian portal. Walled up in the 7th century, the gate has remained closed ever since *(above)*.

6 Ashrafiyya Madrasa
One of several Islamic colleges on the platform, the Ashrafiyya was built in 1482 by Qaitbey and is a masterpiece of Islamic design. The doorway incorporates bands of colored stone, stalactite carvings, and interlocking "joggled" stones *(above)*.

7 El-Kas Fountain
The largest of the fountains still operational in the Haram, the 14th-century El-Kas Fountain *(above)* is carved from a single block of stone.

8 Minbar of Burhan al-Din
This delicate *minbar* (pulpit) by the south *qanatir* is exquisitely carved, and includes some delicate Crusader sculpture. It is used for outdoor services during the summer.

9 Qanatir
A *qanatir* (arcade) tops each of the eight flights of steps leading up to the Dome of the Rock. Some of the column capitals of the arcades were reused from Roman buildings.

10 Sabil of Qaitbey
The carved stone dome of this *sabil* (public fountain), with an interior as finely decorated as its exterior, is unique in the Holy Land. It was built in the 15th century by the Mameluke Sultan Qaitbey, in the shape of a tomb.

Inside the Dome of the Rock
The interior of the dome is lavishly decorated with floral motifs and inscriptions. At the center of the octagon is the Holy Rock, from where Muslims believe Mohammad began his Night Journey, leaving his footprint in the south-west corner. For Jews, the Rock is associated both with Abraham's sacrificial offering of Isaac and as the site of the Holy of Holies. Two octagonal ambulatories allow the faithful to circle the sacred center.

The Citadel (Tower of David)

An imposing fortress dominating the Jaffa Gate entrance to the Old City, the Citadel has been the stronghold of Jerusalem for over 2,000 years. Herod the Great built this monumental edifice to protect his palace, and it is therefore the most probable site of Christ's trial and conviction by Pontius Pilate. The earliest remains here date back to the 2nd century BC, but the present structure is 14th century, with additions made by Suleyman the Magnificent in 1531–2. With a museum illuminating the history of Jerusalem, and stunning views from the ramparts, the Citadel is an ideal starting point for a tour of the Old City.

Gateway to the Citadel

🌀 Take warm clothes to the Night Spectacular as it can get chilly sitting outdoors during the performance.

🍴 The Armenian Tavern is a 2-minute walk from the Citadel along Armenian Patriarch St. It serves drinks and meals in a distinctive underground restaurant (open noon–10pm Mon–Sat).

• Map N4 • Jaffa Gate
• (02) 626 5310/5333
• Egged bus 60 to Jaffa Gate, or Light Rail to Safra Square • Open Sep–Jun: 10am–4pm Sun–Thu, 10am–2pm Sat; Jun–Jul: 10am–5pm Sat–Wed, 10am–6pm Thu, 10am–2pm Fri
• Adults: adm $8; Night Spectacular adults: adm $14; Combined ticket adults: adm $18 • Free guided tours in English 11am Sun–Thu • www.towerofdavid.org.il

Top 10 Features

1. Gateway
2. Museum
3. Minaret
4. Ramparts
5. Model of Jerusalem
6. Mameluke Cupola
7. The Night Spectacular
8. Hasmonean Wall
9. Phasael's Tower
10. The Mosque

Gateway
The ornamental triple-arched gateway was constructed by Suleyman the Magnificent in the 16th century. From its outer steps, British General Allenby declared the liberation of the city from Turkish rule in 1917.

Museum
Within the Citadel is the Tower of David Museum, illustrating the history of Jerusalem through displays, video footage, and dioramas (below). Rooms are arranged chronologically, from the First Temple Period to the end of the British Mandate.

Minaret
Added in 1655, this minaret on the southern edge of the Citadel is known as "the Tower of David." The misnomer harks back to the Byzantines, who wrongly identified this site as the palace of David.

Ramparts

Great views of the city can be enjoyed from the crenellated ramparts *(above)*. Although they date from the 14th century, the walls follow the same lines as they did in Crusader times.

Model of Jerusalem

Displayed in an underground cistern, this model dates from 1873. Created by Hungarian artist Stefan Illes, it provides a record of tho city 140 years ago.

Mameluke Cupola

Part of the Mameluke reconstruction which began in 1310, this little cupola *(below)* sits atop a hexagonal room dating from the same period.

The Night Spectacular

A stunning 45-minute Sound and Light Show *(above)* is organized in the Citadel most evenings. The lighting effects are striking and the music stirring.

Hasmonean Wall

Dating from the 2nd century BC, this curve of Hasmonean city wall was defended by two towers. A further section of the same wall can be seen in the Jewish Quarter.

Phasael's Tower

The immense stone blocks forming the base of this tower are the remains of Herod the Great's original defensive structure, which he named after his brother Phasael.

The Mosque

Built by the Mameluke Sultan Al-Nasir Mohammad, this mosque *(above)* was converted from a Crusader hall. The *minbar* and *mihrab* remain and there are displays on the Islamic history of the city.

The Exhibition Route

The Exhibition Route is one of three signed routes leading visitors around the Tower of David Museum. Highlights to look out for in the East Tower include the model of the City of David in the 10th century BC and the model of Robinson's Arch. In the Southeast Tower there is a fascinating replica of St. Helena's 4th-century Church of the Holy Sepulchre, while in the Crusader Hall, a detailed model of the Dome of the Rock is the centerpiece. The Northwest Tower has a scale reconstruction of a striped stone street that brings Mameluke architecture to life.

Israel Museum

Founded in 1965, the Israel Museum is regarded as one of the world's leading art and archaeology institutions, holding a collection of nearly 500,000 objects spanning prehistory to the present day. An extensive renovation project has doubled the gallery space and created three new glass pavilions to complement the Modernist geometry of the original building. In addition to permanent and temporary exhibition galleries, the museum has a landscaped garden, libraries, an acclaimed restaurant, and cafés.

Mosaic, Archaeology Wing

There are two routes in and out of the main galleries, one via the open-air Carter Promenade and another through the Route of Passage.

Mansfeld, a dairy café, has three branches with some outdoor seating. At the main entrance of the museum, Modern is a restaurant serving non-vegetarian fare.

- Ruppin Blvd., Jerusalem • Map J5
- (02) 670 8811 • Egged buses 9 &14
- Open 10am–5pm Sat– Mon, Wed & Thu; 4–9pm Tue; 10am–2pm Fri
- Adults: adm $13
- Photography is not permitted inside the galleries
- www.imjnet.org.il

Top 10 Features

1. The Shrine of the Book
2. Second Temple Model
3. Ruth Youth Wing
4. Archaeology Wing
5. Jewish Art and Life Wing
6. Library
7. Fine Arts Wing
8. Temporary Exhibition Galleries
9. Gift Shops
10. Billy Rose Art Garden

The Shrine of the Book

Housed in the heart of the Shrine are the oldest biblical manuscripts in the world: the Dead Sea Scrolls. A full-scale facsimile of the Great Isaiah Scroll – the only completely intact scroll found – forms the dramatic centerpiece of the exhibition *(main image)*.

Ruth Youth Wing

Dedicated to interactive art activities, Ruth Youth Wing *(above)* features galleries, art and craft studios, a library of illustrated children's books, and a recycling room. Creative learning also involves parents, and the wing is largely active during school vacations.

Second Temple Model

This scale model covers almost an acre and gives a 3D view of the topography and architecture of Jerusalem in AD 66. The same period is documented by the Dead Sea Scrolls, when Rabbinic Judaism took shape and Christianity was born.

Archaeology Wing

Starting with the anthropoid sarcophagi at the entrance, this chronological journey through the Holy Land never fails to impress. There are fine mosaic floors from Beth Shean and Nablus, as well as priceless treasures from neighboring cultures including Egypt, Greece, and the Islamic world.

Jewish Art and Life Wing

Presenting the culture and art of the Jewish diaspora spanning centuries – from the Middle

Ages to the present day – this wing showcases both sacred *(left)* and secular elements of the Jewish way of life.

Library

The Art and Archaeology Library contains two floors of books and periodicals on architecture, ethnology, costume, ceramics, and much more. The peaceful reading room is awash with natural light.

Fine Arts Wing

This wing contains prints, photos, and design creations alongside traditional paintings and sculpture. Highlights are the Lipchitz Room, the galleries of modern art, and the contemporary art collection *(below)*.

Temporary Exhibition Galleries

These central galleries can house up to three exhibitions at a time. Past exhibitions have included international figures such as William Kentridge and Christian Marclay, as well as renowned Israeli artists.

Gift Shops

Two gift shops *(below)* sell quality products inspired by the museum's collections, including Judaica, jewelry, replicas, and accessories. Prints of paintings are popular.

Billy Rose Art Garden

Designed by artist Isamu Noguchi, this blends elements from Japanese Zen gardens and Western sculpture, with a backdrop of Jerusalem's landscape.

Design of the Shrine of the Book

Inspired by the shape of the lids of the jars in which the Scrolls were found, the Shrine of the Book is a landmark in architectural design. Outside, the white dome contrasts with a black basalt wall, referencing the battle between the Sons of Darkness and the Sons of Light as described in the War Scroll. Jets of water constantly spray the dome's exterior – a symbol of the purity of the desert community who wrote the scrolls nearly 2,000 years ago.

Several free tours are given each day. Pick up a schedule from the information desk at the entrance.

Left *Sea of Galilee* Center **The Rothschild Room** Right *Jeanne Hébuterne, Seated*

Exhibits in the Israel Museum

1 Turning the World Upside Down, Jerusalem (2010)
Anish Kapoor's stainless steel sculpture crowns the museum's highest outdoor point. Standing 16 ft (5 m) high, its polished mirror-like surfaces capture and reverse reflections of the sky and surrounding landscape.

2 Church and Synagogue Bemas
Early Christian and Jewish houses of prayer dating from the 4th to the 7th centuries AD are contrasted in this installation. The synagogue *bema* (chancel) is from Susiya while the church *bema* has marble and stone architectural elements from 17 different churches.

3 Mihrab from Isfahan (17th century)
Inside a mosque, the *mihrab* is the most ornamented section. This specimen is adorned with glazed mosaics – cut from blue tiles – and Quranic verses.

4 Herodian Royal Bath House (1st century)
This reconstructed hot room from Herod's palace is decorated with colorful frescos, tiles, and mosaic floors. Raised on pillars and with earthenware piping built into the walls to provide heating, it was the latest in Roman technology.

5 The Rothschild Room (18th century)
This Parisian salon, donated by Baron Edmond de Rothschild, is hung with tapestries, paintings, chandeliers, and gilt paneling.

6 Leopard Head Hip Mask (17th century)
From Benin in Africa, this pendant was worn by high-ranking officials on their left hip, under a scabbard or sword. The mask is cast in brass and punched with copper studs.

7 St. Peter in Prison (1631)
This painting of St. Peter demonstrates Rembrandt's genius for expressing spiritual qualities through the contrast of light and shadow. The saint sits in a pool of light, while large parts of the canvas are in darkness. Peter's humanity is apparent in his lined face and fisherman's hands, yet the radiance that surrounds him conveys his sanctity.

Key

■ Lower Level

■ Upper Level

Top 10 Highlights

1 20th-century wedding dress from Cochin, India

2 19th-century bridal jewelry from Izmir, Turkey

3 19th-century Hungarian funeral carriage

4 15th-century Maimonides' illuminated Mishne Torah

5 19th-century sukkah from Fishach

6 Shabbat spice boxes

7 18th-century Suriname synagogue

8 120 Hanukkah lamps

9 Esther Scrolls from Purim

10 18th–19th-century hooded cape from Morocco

Jewish Art & Life Wing

This wing comprises treasures associated with Jewish rituals around birth, marriage, and death, and ends with a stunning array of clothing and jewelry from throughout the diaspora. The attention given to aesthetics and presentation, in addition to each object's historical value, makes an immediate impact. Particularly memorable are the two walls displaying over 100 Hanukkah lamps in lit glass cases, and the gallery of rare illuminated manuscripts which includes Maimonides' Mishne Torah from the 15th century. Visitors can follow a Synagogue Route through the reconstructed interiors of synagogues brought from Germany, Italy, India, and Suriname, each one reflecting the culture of its host country while maintaining the key features of a Jewish house of worship.

Hanukkah lamp

The Tzedek ve-Shalom synagogue from Paramaribo in Suriname

8 The Sea of Galilee (mid-1920s)

Reuven Rubin used a naive style and clear colors inspired by Palestine's bright landscapes to capture scenes of daily life. Here he contrasts traditional and modern life, as agriculture meets nature and the Arab and Zionist worlds connect.

9 Jeanne Hébuterne, Seated (1918)

Modigliani's portrait of his pregnant mistress is a classic example of his idealized style – using flowing lines to define her flat oval face, long neck, and almond eyes. When Modigliani died suddenly at the age of 36, a despairing Jeanne killed herself during her ninth month of pregnancy. A Congolese mask is displayed above the portrait, highlighting the influence of African art on the artist.

10 Space That Sees (1992)

In the Billy Rose Art Garden, follow the gravel path down to view James Turrell's Modernist sculpture hewn from the bedrock. Looking through the white frame to a square of blue sky above feels like being inside an abstract painting. After dark, the stars offer another perspective.

🔟 The Mount of Olives

A steep hill on the eastern side of the Old City, the Mount of Olives is venerated as the setting for Christ's agony and betrayal in the Garden of Gethsemane and, later, his Ascension to Heaven. Here Jesus's Last Path leads down to the Via Dolorosa, and many churches commemorate the events of the final week of his life. When seen across the Kidron Valley, with the domes of the Church of St. Mary Magdalene above the glittering mosaic of the Basilica of the Agony, the Mount of Olives makes one of the city's best vistas. Yet it is the view of the Old City from the Mount itself that many travelers count as the finest in Jerusalem.

Tomb of the Virgin

⏰ Some of the churches have restricted opening hours. Tuesday and Thursday mornings are the only times when everything is open.

• Tomb of the Virgin: Map Q4; Open 5am–noon & 2–5pm daily
• Basilica of the Agony: Map Q4; Open 8am–noon & 2:30–5:30pm
• Garden of Gethsemane: Map Q4
• Jewish Cemeteries: Map R5 • Church of St. Mary Magdalene: Map R4; Open 10am–noon Tue, Thu & Sat
• Dominus Flevit Chapel: Map R4; Open 8–11:45am & 2:30–7pm daily • Tombs of the Prophets: Map R4; Open 9:30am–3pm Mon–Thu
• Mosque of the Ascension: Map R4; Open 8am–2:30pm daily (till 5pm summer)
• Russian Church of the Ascension: Open 9am–1pm Tue & Thu
• Church of the Paternoster: Map R4; Open 8:30am–noon & 3–4:45pm Mon–Sat

Top 10 Features

1. Tomb of the Virgin
2. Basilica of the Agony
3. Garden of Gethsemane
4. Jewish Cemeteries
5. Church of St. Mary Magdalene
6. Dominus Flevit Chapel
7. Tombs of the Prophets
8. Mosque of the Ascension
9. Russian Church of the Ascension
10. Church of the Paternoster

1 Tomb of the Virgin

This cruciform underground crypt was cut into solid rock in Byzantine times. Reached via a vaulted Crusader-era stairway, the chamber is venerated as the site of Mary's Tomb, and decorated with ornate lamps in Greek Orthodox style.

3 Garden of Gethsemane

The olive trees *(above)* in the Garden of Gethsemane, next to the Basilica of the Agony, are estimated to be at least 1,000 years old. Christ is said to have prayed in the garden the night before his arrest.

2 Basilica of the Agony

This basilica, designed by Italian architect Antonio Barluzzi, is built over the rock on which it is said Jesus prayed before his arrest. The gilded mosaic on the pediment presents a striking depiction of Christ's agony *(main image)*.

4 Jewish Cemeteries

The Mount of Olives also functions as a burial place. Jewish cemeteries border the Valley of Jehoshaphat, from where it is said mankind will be resurrected on the Day of Judgment.

5 Church of St. Mary Magdalene

The gilded onion domes of this 1885 church *(left)* are one of the most distinctive features of Jerusalem's skyline. There's an icon of the Virgin Mary here, and the bodies of two Russian Orthodox saints lie in glass cabinets on either side of the iconostasis.

6 Dominus Flevit Chapel

Barluzzi designed this chapel in the shape of a teardrop, as the site is identified as the place where Jesus wept over the fate of Jerusalem. The altar window *(above)* frames a beautiful view of the Old City.

7 Tombs of the Prophets

Revered as the tombs of the 5th-century BC prophets – Haggai, Malachi, and Zechariah – these fan-shaped catacombs in fact date from the 1st century AD.

8 Mosque of the Ascension

Since AD 380 this place has been revered as the site of Jesus's Ascension. Now part of a mosque, the medieval chapel here contains Christ's footprint.

9 Russian Church of the Ascension

Orthodox tradition holds that it was from this point on the Mount of Olives that Christ rose to heaven. The church's bell tower is a symbol of the Ascension.

10 Church of the Paternoster

This 19th-century church *(below)* was built above the grotto where Christ taught the disciples the Lord's Prayer (Paternoster). The walls are covered with plaques rendering the prayer in nearly 100 languages.

Up and Down the Mount

It is a tough uphill climb to the top of the Mount, so many people choose to start at the summit and walk down. Taxis wait near the Basilica of the Agony to drive people uphill, and Arab bus 75 starts from near Damascus Gate to Et-Tur village at the top. If walking up, take the road that passes in front of the Church of St. Mary Magdalene – it continues past the main sights and is the least steep route.

🔟 Bethlehem

According to the Old Testament, Bethlehem was home to the shepherd-boy David and also where he was later crowned King of Israel. Of course, it is most famous as the birthplace of Jesus Christ. Emperor Constantine ordered the first church to be built at the site of the Nativity in AD 326, making it the oldest operating church in Christendom. However, because of Palestinian immigration after 1948, Muslims now outnumber Christians in the area. The construction of the separation wall around Bethlehem has done much to damage the economy, though the tourist trade has picked up in recent years.

Manger Square

🚌 Buses for Bethlehem leave from the Arab bus station opposite Damascus Gate in Jerusalem.

- Map F4
- The Milk Grotto: Milk Grotto St.; Open summer: 8am–noon & 4–6pm, winter: 8am–noon & 4–5pm
- Church of the Nativity: Manger Square; Open summer: 5am–7pm, winter: 5am–5pm
- St. Catherine's Church: Manger Square; Open 5:30am–5:30pm daily
- Baituna Al-Talhami: Paul VI St.; (02) 274 2589; Open 8am–noon & 2–5pm Mon–Wed, Fri & Sat; noon–5pm Thu; adm $2
- Palestinian Heritage Center: Manger St.; (02) 274 2381; Open 10am–8pm Mon–Sat
- Rachel's Tomb: Hebron Rd.; Open daily (except Shabbat); Egged bus 163

Top 10 Features

1. The Milk Grotto
2. Church of the Nativity
3. Manger Square
4. St. Catherine's Church
5. Old Market
6. Palestinian Heritage Center
7. Banksy's Graffiti
8. Shepherds' Fields
9. Solomon's Pools
10. Rachel's Tomb

The Milk Grotto
Tradition says this cave sheltered the Holy Family *(main image)* during the Massacre of the Innocents, and that a drop of Mary's milk fell here as she nursed Jesus. A chapel stands here today, its walls covered with testimonials to the site's power to help women conceive.

Church of the Nativity
The cave under this church has been revered as the birthplace of Christ since AD 160 – a silver star marks the spot *(above)*. The church was rebuilt in 530, but many features remain from the original basilica.

Manger Square
Dominated by the walls of the Church of the Nativity and the 1860 Mosque of Omar, Manger Square is the hub of the town. A Swedish-built Peace Center has information for visitors.

St. Catherine's Church
This church was built by the Franciscans in 1882 on the site of a monastery associated with St. Jerome established in the 5th century. His statue is located in the cloisters *(right)*.

Old Market

The atmospheric souk (market) sells traditional olive-wood carvings. The Baituna Al-Talhami museum is here, selling gifts and embroidery made by the Arab Women's Union *(left)*.

Palestinian Heritage Center

Visitors can explore a reconstructed bedouin tent and a Palestinian living room at this center. There is a gift shop on site that sells embroidery created by local women *(above)*.

Banksy's Graffiti

In 2005 and 2007, UK street artist Banksy put 15 images on the separation wall in the West Bank. Many of his iconic artworks can be seen in Bethlehem.

Rachel's Tomb

Rachel was Jacob's wife, and her tomb is always busy with women who come to pray for fertility. The tomb, now separated from Bethlehem by the wall, is the third holiest site in Judaism.

Solomon's Pools

These reservoirs *(above)*, 3 miles (5 km) southwest of Bethlehem, supplied water to Jerusalem from Herod's time until the 20th century. The fort here was built by Suleyman the Magnificent in the 17th century.

Shepherds' Fields

In the village of Beit Sahour, near Bethlehem, is this site *(below)* where the "shepherds watched their flocks by night". Greek and Roman Catholic churches mark where the host of angels appeared.

Christmas in Bethlehem

Christmas Eve in Manger Square is an emotional experience, with Midnight Mass from St. Catherine's Church being broadcast around the world. With all the denominations present in the Holy Land, Christmas celebrations stretch over a long period. Festivities can be enjoyed during the run-up, and masses last until January 18. Information on the timings of services is available from the Christian Information Centre by Jaffa Gate.

TOP 10 Jaffa

Adjoining the southern edge of Tel Aviv but a world away in atmosphere, Jaffa is best reached by strolling along the waterfront promenade. One of the oldest ports in the world, it served as the entry point into Palestine for the first Christian pilgrims and Jewish immigrants but lost much of its importance with the expansion of Tel Aviv in the 1920s. The Ottoman-era architecture and mosques are now being restored, the port's warehouses are morphing into fashionable hangouts, and the process of gentrification is well underway.

Mahmoudiya Mosque

🍃 A new Seaside Park to the south of Jaffa is an impressive "green" initiative.

🍴 Said Abou Elafia and Sons Bakery, near the clock tower, makes takeaway pizza, *sambusa* (stuffed baked pitta) and more.

• Visitors' Center: Kedumim Sq.; Map S6; Open Mar–Nov: 9am–8pm Sun–Thu & Sat, 9am–5pm Fri; Dec–Feb: 9am–5pm Sun–Thu & Sat, 9am–3pm Fri; Adm $2 • Mahmoudiya Mosque: Map T5
• Gan ha-Pisga: Map S6
• Flea Market: Map T6
• Clock Tower: Map T6
• Artists' Quarter: Map S6 • Ilana Goor Museum: 4 Mazal Dagim; Map S6; (03) 683 7676; Open 10am–4pm Sun–Fri, 10am–6pm Sat; Adm $4
• HaTachana: Map T5; www.hatachana.co.il; Shops: open 10am–10pm Sat–Thu, 10am–5pm Fri • Monastery of St. Peter: 1 Mifratz Shlomo, Kedumin Sq.; Map S6; Open 8–11:45am & 3–5pm

Top 10 Features

1. The Mahmoudiya Mosque
2. Gan ha-Pisga
3. Flea Market
4. Yefet Street
5. Clock Tower
6. Artists' Quarter
7. Kedumin Square
8. Port Area
9. HaTachana
10. Monastery of St. Peter

1 The Mahmoudiya Mosque

Dating from 1809–12, this mosque has columns from Caesarea and Ashqelon integrated into its structure. In the south wall is the marbled Suleyman fountain, and further south is a renovated octagonal *sabil*.

3 Flea Market

Jaffa's *Souk HaPishpeshim* (flea market) is a draw in its own right, offering shop, stall, and pavement space to a mixture of outrageous junk and genuine antiques *(above)*. Retro furniture and vintage shops inter-mingle with appealing café-bars.

2 Gan ha-Pisga

This garden stands on the ancient *tel* (mound) of Jaffa, where many archaeological remains have been found. At the pinnacle is the Statue of Faith *(below)*, affording first-rate views of Tel Aviv.

4 Yefet Street

Notable buildings dating from Ottoman times stand at the southern end of this road. Seek out the French Hospital, Emigrant House, and the Urim School for Girls.

Clock Tower

Built at the turn of the 19th century to mark the silver jubilee of Sultan Abdul Hamid II, this clock tower *(left)* incorporates 1960s stained-glass windows and a plaque commemorating Israelis killed in the 1948 battle for Jaffa.

Artists' Quarter

Jaffa's old Arab houses have been converted into studios, galleries, and homes for artists and artisans. Of particular interest among the stone lanes here is the Ilana Goor Museum, housed in what was a *khan* (hostel) for Jewish pilgrims.

Kedumin Square

In this reconstructed square *(above)*, an underground Visitors' Center has Roman-era exhibits and provides tourist information, while restaurants and galleries enliven the outdoor spaces.

Port Area

Jaffa's port area *(main image)* still sees a few fishing vessels set sail, but is best known for its contemporary gallery spaces. The Nalaga'at Center is intriguing – excellent meals are served there by blind waiters in the dark.

HaTachana

The renovated old Jaffa train station *(below)* is now a retail and restaurant complex. Buildings have been restored and make for a pleasant meander.

Monastery of St. Peter

This Roman Catholic monastery and church are built in Latin-American Baroque style *(above)* and stand on the site of a former Crusader castle. Tradition states that the apostle Peter once stayed in the nearby "House of Simon the Tanner."

The Origins of Jaffa's Name

Some Egyptian writings refer to the port city as Yapu, and in biblical sources it is called Joppa. Yet another tradition says it is named after Japheth, son of Noah. Pliny the Elder connected the name with Jopa – daughter of the Greek God of wind. Today, Arabs refer to it as Yaffa and Israelis call it Yafo and believe the name originates from "yofi," the Hebrew word for "beauty."

🔟 Masada

In AD 72–3 at the mountaintop fortress of Masada, 967 Jewish rebels chose mass suicide over submission to the State of Rome. Besieged by Roman legions, the rebels held out for two years before defeat became inevitable and they took their own lives. Although there is evidence that a stronghold existed here in the 2nd century BC, it was Herod the Great who fortified the complex and added two palaces for himself and his family. The Romans took Masada when Herod died, but it was captured by the rebels during the First Jewish Revolt in AD 66. Since its rediscovery, Masada has become a symbol of the modern State of Israel and some units of the IDF hold their swearing-in ceremonies here.

Snake Path

🔄 The Snake Path opens an hour before sunrise.

🍴 A large restaurant and a McDonalds are located at the Masada Visitors' Center. Alternatively, the Aroma café, at the Petra Center in Ein Bokek, is good for light meals and is open 8am to 10pm.

- Map H5 • Off Route 90, 11 miles (18 km) S of Ein Gedi, 9 miles (15 km) north of Ein Bokek • (08) 658 4207
- Egged bus 486 from Jerusalem, buses 486 & 444 back to Jerusalem
- Summer: sunrise–5pm, winter: sunrise–4pm; adm $7 (cable car costs extra) • Yigael Yadin Museum: open 8am–4:30pm; Adm $5 • Sound & Light: (08) 995 9333; Mar–Oct: open 9pm Tue & Thu; Adm $12 • www.parks.org.il

Top 10 Features

1. Sunrise
2. The Hanging Palace
3. The Synagogue
4. Roman Ramp and Camps
5. The Bathhouse
6. Sound and Light Show
7. Snake Path and Cable Car
8. Western Palace
9. Yigael Yadin Museum
10. Water Cisterns

Sunrise
Masada opens at sunrise, when the views from the fortress over the Dead Sea to the Jordanian mountains are particularly stunning. Many groups begin their tour with this early morning vista.

The Hanging Palace
Herod's residence *(above)* was built on three tiers suspended over the northern side of the cliff. The upper level had bedrooms, and a balcony offering Dead Sea views, while the lowest terrace had a bathhouse for the royal family.

The Synagogue
Possibly part of the Herodian construction, this synagogue faced Jerusalem and would have served the rebels during the revolt. They built stone benches along the walls and added the pillars that can still be seen *(below)*.

IDF stands for Israel Defense Forces.

4 Roman Ramp and Camps

On the western side is the huge ramp made by the Romans which enabled them to eventually break Masada's defenses. A siege wall and camps encircling the site were also built; these are still visible today.

5 The Bathhouse

Comprising four rooms and an open court, this bathhouse *(above)* was altered by the rebels, who added immersion pools to many buildings. The *caldarium* (hot bath), with columns supporting the raised floor, is well preserved.

6 Sound and Light Show

Twice a week, March through October, Masada puts on a Sound and Light Show *(below)*, and each June an opera is performed here. Entrance is via Arad only and reservations are essential.

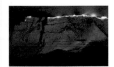

7 Snake Path and Cable Car

The Snake Path to the summit takes at least 45-minutes to climb, so during the day take the cable car up and admire the great views, and then walk back down via the winding path.

8 Western Palace

This palace was used for ceremonial occasions and for accommodating guests. Some of the mosaic floors *(right)* and wall frescoes have survived in an amazing state of preservation.

9 Yigael Yadin Museum

Named in honor of the Israeli archaeologist who excavated Masada in the 1960s, this museum displays finds such as jewelry, coins, and a braid of a woman's hair. The displays are put in context after a visit to the site itself.

10 Water Cisterns

Of the 12 immense cisterns Herod had hewn into the mountainside, the southern cistern is the largest. Rain and flood water was collected below, and brought up the hill to fill the cisterns on top of the rock. This water system is Masada's most important feature.

The Siege of Masada

First-century historian Flavius Josephus wrote of the events at Masada. The Romans besieged the fortress, battering its defenses. As the inner retaining walls burned, the rebels, led by Eleazar ben Ya'ir, realized that defeat was unavoidable and killed their wives and children before killing themselves.

 Most visitors access Masada from the east, via cable car or the Snake Path, but one can easily walk up the Roman Ramp from the west.

🔟 St. Catherine's Monastery

In AD 337, within the shadow of Mount Sinai, Empress Helena built a chapel to mark the spot where Moses saw the Burning Bush. This sanctuary was replaced by the Emperor Justinian with the present-day monastery, which has been under the control of the Greek Orthodox Church ever since. In the following years the impregnable walls of the monastery became a refuge for pilgrims who crossed the desert. In the 10th century, Greek monks claimed to have found the body of the martyr St. Catherine nearby, and the monastery was re-named. It holds religious significance for Jews, Christians, and Muslims alike, and here the three great monotheistic religions meet in peace.

Bell Tower

🕐 Remember to dress modestly. Bare legs and arms are not permitted.

🍴 There's a courtyard café at the Monastery Guesthouse. Relax here with a cup of coffee or a beer. To book a table at the restaurant call (069) 347 0353.

• Map D1 • South Sinai: 1 mile (2 km) from St. Catherine's village (Al-Milga), 56 miles (90 km) W of Dahab and Nuweiba • (069) 347 0343 • One bus to/from Cairo per day to St. Catherine's village. Twice weekly minibus from Dahab and Nuweiba. Most easily visited with a tour group • Open 9–11:45am Mon–Thu & Sat, 11am–noon Fri; closed Sun and Greek Orthodox holidays • Museum: adm • www. sinaimonastery.com

Top 10 Features

1. The Walls
2. Elevated Entrance
3. Bell Tower
4. Museum
5. Basilica of the Transfiguration
6. Mosaic of the Transfiguration
7. The Burning Bush
8. Mosque
9. Gardens and Orchard
10. Charnel House

1 The Walls
The enclosing granite walls *(main image)* are part of the structure built by Emperor Justinian between AD 527 and 62. In places they are 67 ft (20 m) high, with Christian symbols carved into their exterior.

4 Museum
On display here is a selection of the monastery's priceless collection of 2,000 icons *(above)*, which survived the Byzantine Iconoclasm. The museum also contains gifts from cities as diverse as Kolkata and Moscow, as well as examples of manuscripts from the library.

2 Elevated Entrance
Until the 20th century, this tiny raised door was the only access to the monastery. A pulley system lifted visitors and goods so that they could enter the sanctuary.

3 Bell Tower
Built in 1871, this tiered tower contains nine bells donated by Tsar Alexander II of Russia. Nowadays, they are rung only during major religious festivals.

Local police require visitors to pay a guide to accompany them up Mount Sinai.

Basilica of the Transfiguration

This gloriously decorative church has ornate lamps suspended from the ceiling and the air is infused with incense in the Greek Orthodox tradition. The 12 massive pillars are original, while the gilded iconostasis *(above)* dates from 1612.

Mosaic of the Transfiguration

This mosaic in the Basilica's apse depicts the Transfiguration. The earliest mosaic of the Eastern Church, it features Christ in the center, with Moses and Elijah on either side, and Peter, James, and John at his feet.

The Burning Bush

Located outside its namesake chapel, this spiky shrub *(above)* is said to be a direct descendant of the Burning Bush through which God spoke to Moses. An essential photo-stop for pilgrims.

Mosque

This Fatimid mosque was built in 1106 as a shelter for pilgrims en route to Mecca. The white semi-detached minaret stands 33 ft (10 m) high, significantly lower than the church's bell tower.

Gardens and Orchard

The monastery gardens have been nurtured by monks over the centuries, with olive trees and vegetables tended by the small community. The apricot trees bloom for a short period in spring.

St. Catherine the Martyr

According to legend, St. Catherine was martyred in Alexandria in the 4th century for refusing to renounce her Christian faith. Emperor Maxentius had her tortured before beheading her. Her body then vanished, but was transported by angels to the top of Mount Sinai. Six centuries later, it was found by local monks, brought down from the mountain, and placed in a golden casket inside the basilica.

Charnel House

The bones of monks exhumed from the cemetery are placed in this Charnel House. The remains of the archbishops are accorded their own special niches, and the heaps of skulls on display *(above)* are morbidly fascinating to visitors.

🔟 Petra – the Siq

The Siq affords the most dramatic entrance into Petra. This deep narrow gorge, all but shutting out sunlight, twists almost imperceptibly downward until it abruptly opens into a bright square where the Treasury stands in all its glory. Since ancient times, the Siq has led traders and travelers into the heart of the Nabataean world. Modern-day explorers start at the village of Wadi Musa, from where the way leads half a mile through a valley flanked by sandstone hills known as Bab el-Siq – "Gateway to the Gorge." In the Siq itself, the walls are carved with votive niches, a prelude to the abundance of tombs and sculptures fashioned out of the rock face by the Nabataeans all over their hidden city.

Nabataean graffiti

🔗 **Payment is only in Jordanian dinars (JD); credit cards are not accepted. See the website for the admission fee.**

🔗 **Shaded drink stands are dotted around the site.**

• Map B3
• 28 Wadi Musa, Jordan
• 00962 321 57093
• Open summer: 6am–6pm, winter: 6am–4pm • Horse carriages make the 2-mile (4-km) round trip from the park entrance to the Treasury along the Siq. Horses and camels are also available for short rides around the site • Differently abled visitors can arrange in advance for a horse carriage to make the round trip from the park entrance to the basin area • www. petrapark.com

Top 10 Features

1. Visitors' Center
2. Djinn Blocks
3. Bab el-Siq Triclinium
4. Obelisk Tomb
5. Entrance to the Siq
6. Niche Monument
7. Nabataean Pavements
8. Water Channels
9. View of the Treasury
10. Nabataean Graffiti

1 Visitors' Center

The new Visitors' Center sells entry tickets to the site, and arranges licensed guides in various languages. It also provides brochures and maps. A shop here sells Jordanian handicrafts and gifts, some of which are made by a local women's organization.

2 Djinn Blocks

Petra has 26 of these carved stone blocks, which, according to Arabic folklore, housed *djinns* (malevolent spirits), but are probably tower tombs. Three monoliths are located where the Bab el-Siq narrows *(above)*.

3 Bab el-Siq Triclinium

On the south face of the Bab el-Siq, this tomb exhibits the Nabataean Classical style. Like many tombs in Petra, it served as a dining chamber and was used to host feasts in honor of the dead.

A hat, sunscreen, and sunglasses are essential throughout the year. Do not forget to carry your passport.

Obelisk Tomb

This tomb stands above the Triclinium and shows Egyptian influences in the four obelisks *(above)* that line its front.

Nabataean Pavements

Paving stones were laid along the Siq, probably in the 1st century AD. An extensive section is found near the Niche monument.

Water Channels

The Nabataeans were highly skilled hydraulic engineers, and devised sophisticated systems for water conservation and flood prevention. The Siq has two water channels, *(below)* fed by springs to supply Petra with water.

View of the Treasury

As the Siq winds down to its darkest and narrowest point, a sliver in the sandstone gorge suddenly unveils the rose-pink glow of the Treasury *(main image)*. This first view of the monument is a humbling experience.

Nabataean Graffiti

Carved into the walls of the Siq, graffiti and inscriptions demonstrate the literacy of the Nabataeans. Names and greetings in Latin, Greek, and Aramaic reveal the cosmopolitan nature of their society.

Entrance to the Siq

In the past, a monumental arch spanned the entrance to the Siq. It collapsed in 1896, leaving only the remains of the supporting structure and pilasters carved into the rock face *(left)*, best seen on the south side.

Niche Monument

This shrine is carved from a free-standing rock *(below)*. The central niche is bordered by columns and a frieze, and has two Djinn blocks, one of which has eyes and a nose.

The Nabataeans

An ancient Arab tribes-people, the nomadic Nabataeans (3rd century BC–1st century AD) came to control important trade routes across the desert, from Arabia to Mesopotamia. Key to their success was their efficient water storage technique – hidden cisterns located between the oases they controlled allowed them to traverse the arid wilderness. Trade made them wealthy, and their capital city of Petra became a center of cultural exchange.

Left **Israeli soldiers outside Dome of the Rock, Six-Day War** Right **Crusaders capture Jerusalem**

🔟 Moments in History

1 c. 1800 BC: Arrival of the Hebrew Tribes

Excavations in Jericho show that around 10,000 BC, nomadic people settled into farming communities. Several millennia later, Abraham led the early Hebrews into Canaan, where he purchased the Cave of Machpelah in Hebron. This is when the history of the Jews can be said to have begun.

2 587 BC: Babylonian Exile

The Babylonians conquered the Assyrian rulers and captured Jerusalem. The First Temple, built by Solomon, was destroyed and the Ark of the Covenant lost forever. Judean Jews were forced into exile, which strengthened their religious identity.

3 AD 70: Destruction of the Second Temple

Jews returned to Jerusalem under Persian rule and rebuilt their temple in the 6th century BC. Eventually, Herod the Great began a grand reconstruction of the Jewish Temple in 22 BC. This structure was demolished during the Jewish revolt against Roman rule, when the Romans destroyed the city of Jerusalem.

4 638: Islam Arrives

Six years after Mohammad's death, his successor, Caliph Omar, defeated the Byzantines and became the ruler of Palestine. Islam remained the dominant religion for the next 1,300 years, and the Dome of the Rock and

Caliph Omar arrives in Jerusalem

El-Aqsa Mosque were erected on the Temple Mount. Entry to the "sacred precinct" was forbidden to non-Muslims.

5 1099: Crusaders Capture Jerusalem

Launched in 1095, the Crusades aimed to seize the Holy Land from the Muslims. It took four years for the Crusaders to create a Kingdom of Jerusalem, but true dominance was never achieved. Saladin retook Jerusalem in 1187, and the Crusaders were ousted when Akko fell in 1291.

6 1516: The Ottomans defeat the Mamelukes

The Mamelukes ruled for about 250 years, a period that saw great architectural reconstruction. The Ottomans' victory was the start of their 400-year rule.

7 1922: The Balfour Declaration

Turkish rule came to an end when British troops took Jerusalem in 1917. The Balfour Declaration stated that the British Government "favourably views the creation of a national

Preceding pages **Mosaic, Dome of the Rock**

Jewish home in Palestine". Trans-Jordan was created the following year to appease the Arabs.

8 1948: Declaration of the State of Israel

Following the violence between Jews and Arabs because of Jewish immigration before World War II, the British put the "Palestine Question" before the UN. It was voted to partition the Holy Land, and the British pulled out on May 15, 1948. One day before, Ben-Gurion had declared the birth of the State of Israel.

9 1967: Six-Day War

From 1949 to 1967, Jerusalem was divided along the Green Line, between Israel and Jordan. The Six-Day War saw the Israelis launch a preemptive strike and capture the Golan, the Sinai, the Gaza Strip, the West Bank, and East Jerusalem.

Citizens mourning statesman Yitzhak Rabin

10 1994: Palestinians Granted Limited Autonomy

The Oslo Accords were signed in 1993, allowing the Palestinian Authority (PA) to govern West Bank towns and cities. In 1994 Jordan and Israel signed a historic peace treaty. Since then, Rabin's assassination, the Second Intifada, the West Bank Barrier, and the rise of Hamas have stalled the peace process.

Top 10 Biblical and Historical Figures

1 Moses (c. 1250 BC)
Judaism's most important prophet, Moses led the Exodus, and received the Ten Commandments from God.

2 King David (c. 1004–965 BC)
After capturing Jerusalem, David made it the Israelite capital of a large empire.

3 Herod the Great (c. 73 BC– AD 4)
Herod was appointed King of Judea by the Romans, and his great construction works are still scattered across the land.

4 Jesus (c. 2 BC– AD 30)
Christians believe he was the Son of God, who died on the cross and was resurrected.

5 Rabbi Akiva (AD 50–135)
One of Judaism's greatest scholars, Rabbi Akiva was killed by the Romans for his part in the Bar Kochba Revolt.

6 Baldwin I (c. 1100–1118)
Crowning himself "King of Jerusalem" in the Church of the Nativity on Christmas Day, French King Baldwin was merciless to his enemies.

7 Saladin (c. 1138–1193)
He drove the Crusaders from the Holy Land and is noted for his honor in battle.

8 David Ben-Gurion (1886–1973)
The first prime minister of the independent State of Israel.

9 Yitzhak Rabin (1922–95)
Rabin was assassinated by a right-wing radical, a year after winning the Nobel Peace Prize.

10 Yasser Arafat (1929–2004)
Leader of the PLO, Arafat fought for years to liberate Palestine, but was a key player in later peace negotiations.

Left **Memorial at Yad Vashem** Center **Design Museum Holon** Right **Bible Lands Museum**

TOP 10 Museums

1 Yad Vashem

This memorial to the six million Jews who died in the Holocaust makes a lasting impression. It contains more than 20 memorials, an art museum, and the Avenue of the Righteous Among the Nations – a tribute to the people who risked their own lives to protect Jews. ◎ *Har Hazikaron, near Mount Herzl, Jerusalem • Map F4 • www.yadvashem.org.il*

2 Eretz Israel Museum

The pavilions of Eretz Israel are built around Tel Qasile, an excavated mound revealing 12 eras of human occupation. Also on view is a rare collection of glassware, beautiful Judaica, and mosaic floors from Beit Guvrin *(see p63)*. ◎ *2 Haim Levanon, Ramat Aviv, Tel Aviv • Map X1 • Adm • www. eretzmuseum.org.il*

3 Bible Lands Museum

Outstanding archaeological finds and antiquities, reflecting the various cultures of the Holy Land during biblical times, are displayed in this museum. The exhibits illustrate the influence of the different civilizations on each other. ◎ *25 Avraham Granot St., Givat Ram, Jerusalem • Map J5 • Adm • www.blmj.org*

4 L. A. Mayer Museum of Islamic Art

This museum holds unique Indian Mughal miniatures, examples of calligraphy, and Iranian tiles. There is also a collection of clocks and watches that was stolen over 25 years ago but recently returned; it includes Marie Antoinette's watch. ◎ *2 HaPalmach St., Talbiya, Jerusalem • Map L6 • Adm • www.islamicart.co.il*

5 Tikotin Museum of Japanese Art

Felix Tikotin gifted his private art collection to Haifa over 40 years ago, and now the permanent displays of Japanese master-pieces are augmented with temporary exhibitions. In the Japanese tradition, beautiful objects, including lacquerware, ceramics, and prints, are displayed in harmony with the season. ◎ *89 Hanassi, Haifa • Map C3 • Adm • www.tmja.org.il*

6 Israel Museum

The Israel Museum holds the largest collection of biblical archaeological finds anywhere in the world. The priceless works of art span pre-

Tikotin Museum of Japanese Art

history to the modern day. Since it was founded in 1965, donations and purchases have added to its collections tenfold (*see pp14–17*).

7 Beit Hatfutsot (Museum of the Jewish People)

A thematic museum with interactive displays, dioramas, and videos that reveal life in the Jewish Diaspora. Do not miss the 18 models of synagogues from countries as diverse as China, Syria, and Italy.
🅢 *Gate 2 University of Tel Aviv, Ramat Aviv, Tel Aviv • Map X1 • Adm • www.bh.org.il*

8 Design Museum Holon

Artwork, Tel Aviv Museum of Art

Hosting three international exhibitions each year, this museum, designed by Ron Arad, is the pinnacle of Holon's urban regeneration program. Five iconic rust-colored steel ribbons encircle the building. There are two galleries, a lab for interaction with local design students, plus a café and a shop. The museum is closed between exhibitions, so check the website before visiting. 🅢 *8 Pinhas Eilon St., Holon • Map E3 • Adm • www.dmh.org.il*

Tel Aviv Museum of Art

9 Tel Aviv Museum of Art

Israel's finest collection of art spans the 17th century to the present day, and includes works by Chagall, Degas, Monet, Picasso, and Rothko. The Amir Building is an arresting geometrical edifice with three of its five floors underground. The Helena Rubinstein Pavilion, nearby, is free to enter, and displays changing contemporary art exhibitions. 🅢 *27 Shaul Hamelekh, Tel Aviv • Map X2 • Adm • www.tamuseum.com*

10 Yitzhak Rabin Center

Using state-of-the-art museum technology to tell the story of the birth of the State of Israel, this museum provides a compelling and relatively neutral account of the events culminating in the death of Yitzhak Rabin. There are no artifacts on display here, just footage from the times it describes, leading to a candle-lit room dedicated to Rabin's memory. 🅢 *14 Haim Levanon, Ramat Aviv, Tel Aviv • Map W1 • Adm • www.rabincenter.org.il*

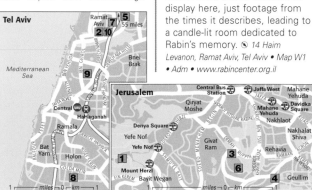

Left **Holon Children's Museum** Right **Jerusalem Biblical Zoo**

Children's Attractions

1 Jerusalem Biblical Zoo

There's a special focus on species mentioned in the Bible at this zoo, hence the name. The facility also houses red pandas, tigers, elephants, penguins, and spider monkeys. ◈ *1 Aharon Shulov St., Jerusalem • Map F4 • Adm • www.jerusalemzoo.org.il/len/*

2 Hezekiah's Tunnel

This amazing tunnel underneath the City of David was hacked out of the bedrock by King Hezekiah to supply water to Jerusalem. Kids adore wading through the thigh-high water in the dark. ◈ *City of David, Jerusalem • Map Q5 • Adm • www.cityofdavid.org.il*

3 Bloomfield Science Museum

This small museum warrants a detour for its interactive exhibits. There are engaging displays on architecture, gravity, electricity, and communications. ◈ *Givat Ram, Jerusalem • Map J4 • www.mada.org.il*

4 Dolphin Reef

Swim with a pod of bottle-nosed dolphins, or observe them from the floating piers. There's a lovely beach with loungers, a restaurant, and a children's activity center. ◈ *South Beach, Eilat • Map C2 • (08) 630 0111 • Open 9am–5pm Sun–Thu, 9am–4:30pm Fri & Sat • Adm*

5 Israel Children's Museum

Devoted to broadening young minds, this museum encourages interactive participation. Sight-and-hearing impaired guides conduct tours that leave a lasting impression on the children. ◈ *1 Mifratz Shlomo St., Peres Park, Holon • Map E3 • 1599 585 858 • Call ahead to book in advance*

6 Old City Ramparts Walk

The Ramparts Walk offers lots of steps, nooks, and gates for exploration, which kids will love. Parents, meanwhile, can enjoy spectacular views of the Old City. ◈ *Map P4*

Bloomfield Science Museum

Mini Israel
Tremendously enjoyable for children, Mini Israel allows them to see the country in miniature. There are about 400 scale models, some of which are dynamic. *Latrun, off Rd. 1 • Map F3 • 1700 599 599 • Adm • www.minisrael.co.il*

Scale models, Mini Israel

Luna Gal Water Park
Israel's oldest water park is located on the eastern edge of the Sea of Galilee, and is suitable even for toddlers. Entry also allows access to the beach, and there are kayaks and inner tubes for hire. *Golan Beach • Map B6 • (04) 667 8000/8/9 • Adm*

Alpaca Farm
Alpacas and llamas are reared here along with horses, camels, donkeys, and sheep. Supervised wool-weaving activities are organized for kids and there's horseback riding around the crater of Makhtesh Ramon. *Mitspe Ramon, the Negev • Map A2 • (08) 658 8047 • Adm • www.alpaca.co.il*

Kings' City
This amusement palace has a boat ride through the life of King Solomon, a 4D Journey to the Past of the Pharaohs, and interactions with biblical stories. The best section is the "Cave of Illusions." *Eilat • Map C2 • (08) 630 4444 • Adm • www.kingscity.co.il*

Top 10 Free Sights

Knesset
The Parliament has guided tours on Sunday and Thursday. *Qiryat Ben-Gurion, Jerusalem • Map J4 • www.knesset.gov.il*

Supreme Court
The court building incorporates emblems relating to justice. *Qiryat Ben-Gurion, Jerusalem • Map J3 • www.court.gov.il*

Yad Vashem
A most poignant museum, Yad Vashem evokes memories of the Holocaust *(see p34)*.

Brigham Young (Mormon) University
The BYU hosts free concerts on Sunday evenings. Book in advance. *Near Augusta Victoria Hospital, Jerusalem • Map R2 • (02) 626 5621*

Sandemans Tours
Staff wearing red t-shirts at Jaffa Gate lead free tours of the Old City. *www.newjerusalemtours.com*

Jerusalem Bird Observatory
This eco-project has utilized a derelict urban space to create a bird-watching center. *Givat Ram, Jerusalem • Map K4 • (02) 653 7374*

Western Wall Plaza
Seeing the faithful at the Western Wall is a magical experience. *Map P4*

View from the Austrian Hospice
The roof of the hospice offers a great view of the Dome of the Rock. *37 Via Dolorosa, Old City, Jerusalem • Map P4*

Baha'i Gardens
These beautiful terraced gardens contain the golden Shrine of the Bab. *45 Yefe Nof S., Haifa • Map C3 • www.ganbahai.org.il*

Reuben and Edith Hecht Museum
Visit the archaeology collection on the "Land of Israel." *University of Haifa • Map C3 • (04) 825 7773*

Left **Altar, Church of the Holy Sepulchre** Right **Monastery of the Flagellation**

Churches and Monasteries

1 St. James's Cathedral

Jerusalem's most beautiful church dates to the 11th century and is built over the tomb of St. James the Apostle, whose severed head lies in the third chapel on the left. The Chapel of Etchmiadzin contains 12th-century Turkish tiles. ⊗ *Armenian Quarter • Map P5 • (02) 628 2331 • Open 3–3:30pm daily; 6:30–7:30am Mon–Fri & 6:30–9:30am Sat*

2 Church of the Holy Sepulchre

Different Eastern and Western Christian sects administer various areas within the Church of the Holy Sepulchre. Don't miss the tiny Coptic chapel, at the rear of the Sepulchre itself *(see pp8–9)*.

3 Basilica of the Agony

Donations from 12 countries enabled the construction of this church. The glittering mosaic above the portico is awe-inspiring, while the cool purple light inside has a calming effect. The plan of the Byzantine church is traced on the floor in black marble, and sections of the original mosaic floor can be viewed beneath glass panels *(see p18)*.

4 St. Anne's Church

Adjacent to Lions' Gate, this Crusader church retains its original Romanesque structure, despite Saladin turning it into a *madrasa* in 1192. The church is the birthplace of the Virgin Mary and steps lead to a crypt said to be the remains of her parents' house. Outside is the Pool of Bethesda, where Jesus healed a paralyzed man. ⊗ *Muslim Quarter • Map Q3 • (02) 628 3285 • Closed noon–2pm • Adm to Pool of Bethesda*

Chapel of the Flagellation

5 Monastery of the Flagellation

The 1929 Chapel of the Flagellation, designed by Antonio Barluzzi, is to the right on entering the complex. Christ was flogged here before he was crucified. Across the courtyard is the Chapel of the Condemnation, where Pontius Pilate is said to have made his judgment. ⊗ *Muslim Quarter • Map P3 • (02) 627 0444 • Closed 11:45am–2pm*

6 Monastery of the Cross

Located in a barren valley ringed by highways, this fortress-like monastery sits in a time-warp that few tourists discover.

Basilica of the Agony

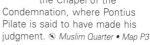

It marks the site of the tree used to make Jesus's cross. The interior has exceptional frescoes, remnants of a Byzantine mosaic floor, a refectory table upstairs, and a little museum. ◎ *Shota Rustaveli St., Neve Granot, Jerusalem • Map K5 • (052) 221 5144 • Open 10am–4:30pm Mon–Sat • Adm*

Church of the Nativity

This church is entered through the tiny Door of Humility, reduced to its present size during the Ottoman period to prevent looters from riding inside on horseback. Within the nave, Crusader paintings of saints appear on 30 of the 44 pink lime-stone columns. Steps lead down to the Grotto of the Nativity, which has the Star of Bethlehem laid in its floor *(see pp20–21).*

Church of the Transfiguration

This "high mountain apart" has been identified with Christ's Transfiguration since the 4th century. Various churches and fortresses have stood here in the intervening centuries, but the present Franciscan structure dates from 1924 and is, again, the work of Barluzzi. A viewpoint offers great vistas of the Galilee. ◎ *Mount Tabor, Galilee • Map C5 • Open 8–11:45am & 2–5pm Sun–Fri*

Basilica of the Annunciation

Basilica of the Annunciation

The largest church in the Middle East, this is the traditional scene of the Annunciation, when the angel Gabriel revealed to Mary that she would be the mother of Christ the Savior. The apse of a 5th-century church encloses a sunken grotto, and is backed by the remains of a Crusader church. Above it all soars the modern edifice, consecrated in 1969. ◎ *Casa Nova St., Nazareth • Map C4 • (04) 655 4170 • Open 8am–6pm*

St. Catherine's Monastery

The buttressed walls of this monastery in Egypt were constructed in the 6th century, and have since sheltered a community of Eastern Orthodox monks. Within the compound, the magnificent Basilica of the Transfiguration is supported by 12 granite pillars decorated with icons of saints, the capitals of which are carved with Christian symbols *(see pp26–7).*

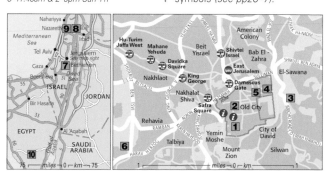

Left **Mul Yam** Right **Diners at Herbert Samuel**

Restaurants in Israel

1 Machne Yuda, Jerusalem
This restaurant cooks up Mediterranean cuisine using fresh ingredients, with the menu changing weekly depending on the season. A split-level space, it is furnished in a country kitchen style, with checkered napkins on the tables and shelves loaded with wine and produce *(see p61)*.

2 Chakra, Jerusalem
Chakra has a circular interior with modish black furniture, white walls, and accents of gold. The meat and fish dishes have an Italian base, augmented by local flavors *(see p61)*.

The bar at Chakra

3 Raphael, Tel Aviv
Arguably Israel's best chef, Raphi Cohen is known for his fusion of Moroccan cooking with French techniques, creating a distinctive Mediterranean flavor. Raphael is also the place to sample the "New Israeli Cuisine,"

which uses eggplant, tomato, yogurt, *tahini*, local herbs, chickpeas and *friki* (roasted green cracked wheat), as well as fresh fish and meat *(see p75)*.

4 Catit, Tel Aviv
Chef Meir Adoni's techniques of molecular-fusion cooking result in extremely creative and complicated courses. The strongest influence on the cuisine comes from Adoni's North African roots. Catit is one of Israel's most expensive restaurants, but there are some good value lunch deals *(see p75)*.

5 Herbert Samuel, Tel Aviv
The menu here is an exemplar of the "New Israeli Cuisine," with a mix of Mediterranean, ethnic, French, and Italian influences. Many dishes come in tapas-sized portions and prices are reasonable *(see p75)*.

6 Brasserie, Tel Aviv
Serving unfussy French food, Brasserie attracts a diverse crowd, is open 24/7, and has a popular breakfast and weekend brunch menu. The continental-style interior and covered terrace are both perfect spots for a relaxed meal *(see p75)*.

7 The Dining Hall, Tel Aviv
Located in the courtyard of the Tel Aviv Performing Arts Center, The Dining Hall has front terraces shaded by white cloth umbrellas, while inside there's

a well-stocked bar. The modern interior, with rectangular tables and plain crockery, is a throwback to the kibbutz dining halls *(heder ochel)* of the past and the food is delicious *(see p75)*.

Mul Yam, Tel Aviv

This sophisticated restaurant specializes in fish and seafood imported from around the world. Located in the renovated Old Port area, with a classic decor, Mul Yam has an extremely expensive à la carte menu, but the business lunch deal is much more affordable *(see p75)*.

Mul Yam

Diana, Nazareth

This restaurant offers the best of local Arabic cooking – it embraces the distinctive Galilean cuisine, and is especially regarded for its *kebabs*, lamb dishes, and *meze*. Chef Dohol Safedi cooks the same dishes as his father before him *(see p81)*.

El Babur, Galilee

The *meze*, baked *kebabs*, and *malabi* (milk pudding) are the specialties of this unpretentious restaurant, which has two branches. Chef Hussam Abbas' courses are visually impressive and include giant plates of *mansaf* (marinated lamb on rice), and vegetable dishes blending eggplant with yogurt, or zucchini stuffed with rice *(see p81)*.

Top 10 Wineries and Breweries

1 Carmel Winery

Founded by Baron Rothschild in 1882, Carmel is known for its Mizrachi Private Collection. ✪ *Winery St., Zichron Ya'akov • Map C3*

2 Golan Heights Winery

Yarden is its premier label and the Cabernet Sauvignon is highly rated. Also try the Golan and Gamla labels, or the Katzrin Chardonnay Classic. ✪ *Katsrin, Golan Heights • Map B6*

3 Margalit

This family-owned business is notable for its Cabernet Franc and Enigma labels. ✪ *Caesarea • Map C3*

4 Barkan

Famed chiefly for its Cabernet Sauvignon wines. ✪ *Kibbutz Hulda • Map F3*

5 Clos de Gat

These vineyards produce the Sycra collection, of which the Muscat is highly rated. ✪ *Ayalon Valley • Map F3*

6 Domaine du Castel

Sample this family-run winery's Castel Grand Vin. ✪ *Ramat Raziel • Map F4*

7 Yatir Winery

Part-owned by Carmel, this small winery has the Yatir Forest as its flagship series. ✪ *Arad • Map H4*

8 Taybeh Brewery

The only Palestinian beer, Taybeh is a golden German-style brew. ✪ *Taybeh village, near Ramallah • Map F4*

9 Tempo Brewery

Tempo brew Israel's market leader Goldstar, and Maccabee, both of which are lagers. ✪ *Natanya • Map D3*

10 Golan Brewery Pub

Four boutique beers are brewed on site in this pub. ✪ *Katsrin, Golan Heights • Map B6*

Left **Falafel** Center **Baklava** Right *Shakshuka*

Regional Dishes

1 Meze or Salatim

Meals begin with a salad spread – *salatim* to Israelis or *meze* to Arabs. Hummus is, of course, the best-loved dish, but close contenders are *labane* (yogurt), *baba ghanoush* (eggplant dip), and *fattoush* (pitta bread salad), while olives and pickles invariably make an appearance.

Sabich

Hummus and pitta

2 Falafel

The ultimate street food, falafel is a favorite with budget travelers. In Israel, falafels are delicious as well as affordable, and the pitta comes stuffed with salad, coleslaw, and hummus, plus a dribble of *amba* (mango sauce) too. In Egypt, falafel is known as *taamiyya*.

4 Shakshuka

An Israeli classic, this dish of eggs poached in a rich tomato, pepper, and onion sauce, has its roots in North Africa, and is also a staple on Egyptian menus. Locals usually eat it for breakfast, but it is good to have at any time – even as a main course. ◈ *Dr Shakshuka: 3 Beit Eshel St., Jaffa*

3 Sabich

This Iraqi sandwich contains potato, *tahini*, salad, spices, and parsley, but the key ingredients are fried eggplant and a hard-boiled egg. When in Tel Aviv head to Sabich Frishman, or to the famed Oved Sabich for a taste. ◈ *Sabich Frishman: 42 Frishman St.; Oved Sabich: 7 Sirkin St., Gavatayim*

5 Malawach and Jahnoun

Brought to Israel by Yemeni immigrants, *malawach* is a panfried bread served with a grated-tomato dip, hard-boiled eggs, and a spicy sauce. The same accompaniments enhance *jahnoun*, a slow-baked bread roll. Both make for a heavy meal.

6 Kibbe/Kubbe

These little croquettes are made of bulgur wheat and minced meat (usually lamb), mixed with onions and pine nuts. A staple in Iraqi-Jewish and Palestinian cuisine, and widely available in Egypt and Jordan, they come shaped as balls or torpedos. Usually served as *meze*.

7 Kebab and Shashlik

In the Middle East, *kebab* refers to meat (usually lamb) which has been ground and spiced, and then grilled on a skewer, while *shashlik* is chunks of meat cooked the same way. Israelis grill on a *mangal* (barbeque), and families head out on holidays to "mangal" together. *Shawarma* is the local, often turkey-based, version of a gyro.

Baklava
A plate of *baklava*, in all its different shapes and colors, is an intrinsic image of the Middle East. The layers of crisp filo pastry and honey-soaked chopped nuts are made even stickier by syrup. Anyone with a serious sweet tooth should look out for sweet shops in the Old City, Nazareth, and Haifa.

Schnitzel
Ashkenazi Jews of German and Austrian origin brought the schnitzel with them and now it's omnipresent. Chicken or turkey is pounded thin, coated in breadcrumbs, and pan-fried. You find it in fast-food places, crammed into pitta with salads, or dressed-up with sesame seeds, spices, and garlic in fancy restaurants.

Knafeh
This Palestinian pastry is loved by all. Large platters of gooey sweet cheese, coated in crunchy pastry and drizzled with a sugary rose syrup, are chopped into slices and sprinkled with color. Best had when it is fresh and hot.

Plates of *knafeh*

Top 10 Places for Hummus

1 Abu Shukri
Known for their sour, light hummus. ✆ *63 Al-Wad St., Muslim Quarter, Jerusalem • Open 8am–4.30pm Mon–Fri*

2 Ta'ami
This place is recommended for their hummus with meat. ✆ *3 Shamai St., nr. Zion Sq., West Jerusalem • Open 9am–6pm Sun–Thu, 9am–3pm Fri*

3 Ha'Suri (The Syrian)
Ask for the hummus with *fuul* (mashed fava beans) and egg. ✆ *27 Malan St., Yemenite Quarter, Tel Aviv • Open 7am–2pm Sun–Fri*

4 Abu Marwan
This authentic local place also does great grilled eggplant. ✆ *129 Yefet St., Jaffa*

5 Abu Hassan
Try the *masabacha* (hummus with a touch of lemon and paprika, sprinkled with whole chickpeas). ✆ *1 Dolphin St., Jaffa • Open 8am–3pm Sun–Fri*

6 As-Sheikh
They serve a delicate hummus, with local olives. ✆ *Afifi Building, Iksal St. (off Paul VI St.), Nazareth • Open 8am–2pm Mon–Sat*

7 Emad's Hummus
The long opening hours are a bonus. ✆ *Taufik Ziad St., Nazareth • Open 5am–7pm daily*

8 Abou Maroun
This place is the pride of Haifa. ✆ *1 Kibbutz Galuyot St., Wadi Salib, Haifa • Open 8am–4pm daily*

9 Humous Sa'eid
Undoubtedly the best in Akko, they also have good *fuul*. ✆ *Benjamin of Tuleda St., Market, Old City, Akko • Open 6am–2:30pm Sun–Fri*

10 Abou Adham
People drive from Tel Aviv just to taste the hummus here. ✆ *Kafr Yasif, off Rd. 70, 7 miles (11 km) northeast of Akko • Open 8am–5pm daily*

Above **Cyclists in the Galilee**

Outdoor Activities

Cycling
Israel offers diverse options for cyclists and mountain bikers as new trails open up, particularly in the Negev. Makhtesh Ramon has challenges for all levels and the green, hilly area of the Galilee is another top destination.
www.ibike.co.il • www.geofun.co.il
• www.hooha.co.il

Horse-Riding
There are many stables in the Galilee, where the rolling hills and cool air add to the fantastic views. In Sinai, several of the large hotels in Sharm el-Sheikh and Dahab offer riding. *www. veredhagalil.co.il • www.alpaca.co.il*

Snorkeling in Eilat

Matkot
An Israeli obsession, this game involves wooden bats and a squash ball, and only requires you to maintain the longest volley possible. Tel Aviv's beaches are thronged with players during the weekends, and sets are available at shops on the promenade.

Playing *matkot* on a beach, Tel Aviv

Diving and Snorkeling
The clear waters, colorful corals, and wealth of marine life along the Gulf of Aqaba mean Sinai and Eilat are among the world's top diving spots. The reefs around Dahab are great for snorkelers, while in Eilat you can "snuba" – a cross between diving and snorkeling. *www.snuba.co.il*
• www.oonasdiveclub.com • www. inmodivers.de

Bird-Watching
Located on the main migration route between Africa and Europe, Israel is the perfect place for birders. Eilat and Lotan eco-kibbutz in the Negev are good bases, and in the Galilee, the Hula Nature Reserve is famed. *www.eilat-birds.org • www. kibbutzlotan.com • www.parks.org.il*

Trekking
Israel boasts an extensive network of marked trails. Guided hikes around Petra can be arranged at the visitors' center, and you can explore the mountains around St. Catherine's Monastery with bedouin guides.
SPNI: 13 Helena HaMalka St., Jerusalem; (02) 625 7682; www.teva.org.il • www.sheikhmousa.com • www. walkingpalestine.com

Rock Climbing
The south of Israel offers many climbing and rappelling opportunities, though these are best done in winter. Tur Canyon

Society for the Protection of Nature in Israel (SPNI) Field Schools are a good source of trekking advice.

is adventurous, and the Upper Rachaf Canyon involves seven descents. In the Golan, the Black Canyon in Zavitan and Yehudia Canyon are rewarding, as are the many valleys of Jordan. ⬧ *www.mountainguides.co.il*

Rock climbing

Skiing
The slopes of Mount Hermon are covered with snow from December to April, although the center is open year round for people to ride the cable cars. In winter, skiing lessons are available and you can hire equipment. ⬧ *www.skihermon.co.il*

Desert Safaris
Some excellent enterprises in the Negev offer camel trips along the old caravan trails of the spice route. The deserts of south Sinai have many *wadis* and secret oases, some of which can be accessed only by camel. Trips can be arranged in St. Catherine's, Nuweiba, or Dahab. ⬧ *www.cameland.co.il • www.camel-riders.com • www.beerotayim.co.il • www.desertfoxsafari.com*

Watersports
There are decent surfing spots in Tel Aviv and other beaches on the Mediterranean. In Sinai, wind- and kite-surfing benefits from the strong breezes, particularly on the west coast, although Dahab also has a lively scene. ⬧ *www.moonbeachholidays.com*

Top 10 Treks

1 Red Canyon
Enjoy a 1½- to 2½-hour trek down this colorful canyon. ⬧ *Off Rd. 12, N of Eilat • Egged bus 392*

2 Mount Shlomo
This long hike affords terrific views from the top of the mountain over the Red Sea and Sinai. ⬧ *Off Rd. 12, N of Eilat • Egged bus 392*

3 Makhtesh Ramon
Start hiking from Mitspe Ramon to get to the crater; maps are available at the information center *(see p84)*.

4 Ein Ovdat National Park
The Nahal Zin trail here has some stunning pools and picnic spots *(see p84)*.

5 Ein Gedi Nature Reserve
Most people only visit the David Falls, but if you have time, attempt the stunning Dry Canyon hike *(see p83)*.

6 Jesus Trail
Follow in Jesus's footsteps past Tsipori *(see p80)* to the Arbel cliff, and behold stunning views of the Sea of Galilee. ⬧ *www.jesustrail.com*

7 Yehudiya Reserve
This trek involves swimming across deep pools. Not recommended in winter. ⬧ *Off Rd. 87, Lower Golan • www.parks.co.il*

8 Golan Trail
A 75-mile (125-km) trek taking at least seven days. Spring is the best time to go. ⬧ *Mount Hermon to Ein Taufik • www.golantrail.com*

9 Israel National Trail
Trek across the country for at least 45 days, covering 625 miles (1,000 km). ⬧ *Northern border to the Gulf of Eilat*

10 Mount Catherine
The 5- to 6-hour climb is rewarded with lovely views. ⬧ *Sinai, Egypt*

Left **Chelouche Gallery** Center **Museum on the Seam** Right **Suzanne Dellal Centre**

Cultural Venues

1 Jerusalem Theatre

This Modernist building is home to the Jerusalem Symphony Orchestra. It is the largest cultural venue in the city, with four performance halls that host musical events, art exhibitions, and movie screenings.
⊗ *20 David Marcus St., Jerusalem • Map L6 • www.jerusalem-theatre.co.il*

Tel Aviv Performing Arts Center

2 Tel Aviv Performing Arts Center (TAPAC)

Home to the Israeli Opera, Philharmonic Orchestra, and National Ballet, the TAPAC boasts state-of-the-art facilities. The on-site Cameri Theatre stages around 10 new productions every year. ⊗ *19 Shaul HaMelech Blvd., Tel Aviv • Map X2 • www.israel-opera.co.il*

3 Zappa Club

The Zappa enterprise puts on live gigs at its atmospheric Jerusalem venue – a warehouse at the old train station. New local talent and international acts are featured, and drinks and dinner are served during performances.
⊗ *28 Hebron Rd., Old Train Station, Jerusalem • (02) 629 2001 • Map N6 • Call ahead for opening times • Adm*

4 Museum on the Seam

Israel's socio-political reality finds expression in the exhibits at this museum. The bullet-scarred building sits on the former Green Line and was once the Tourjeman Post – the last outpost occupied by the Israeli army from 1948–67.
⊗ *4 Chel Handasa St., Jerusalem • Map N2 • Adm • www.mots.org.il*

5 Jerusalem Artists' House

The former home of the Bezalel School of Art, a Jewish arts and crafts movement founded in 1906, this Islamic-style building hosts top-notch art exhibitions.
⊗ *12 Shmuel HaNagid St., Jerusalem • Map L4 • www.art.org.il*

6 Al-Kasaba Theatre and Cinematheque

An active communal space, this complex in Ramallah holds theater productions for adults and children. Movies are screened daily, and there is a gallery space for art exhibitions. The resto-bar is a popular watering hole. ⊗ *Hospital St., near Manara Sq, Ramallah • Map F4 • www.alkasaba.org/english.php*

7 Ticho House

Artist Anna Ticho's house is an oasis in the city, displaying her lovely sketches as well as hosting temporary exhibitions. The Little Jerusalem dairy restaurant in the garden is a charming spot. ⊗ *7 HaRav Kook St., Jerusalem • Map M3 • www.imjnet.org.il*

8 Suzanne Dellal Centre

Home to the Bat Sheva Dance Company, a mainstay of the Israeli contemporary dance scene, the Suzanne Dellal Centre is an important venue. It's a gorgeously renovated Ottoman building located in Neve Tzedek.
◈ 5 Yechieli St., Neve Tzedek, Tel Aviv • Map U5 • www.suzannedellal.org.il

9 Chelouche Gallery for Contemporary Art

This gallery is housed in the "Twin House," Tel Aviv's finest example of 1920s neo-classical architecture. Contemporary mediums such as film, as well as more traditional painting techniques, are introduced here.
◈ 7 Maze St., Tel Aviv • Map V4
• www.chelouchegallery.com

10 Cinematheques

Tel Aviv, Jerusalem, and Haifa all have vibrant cinematheques. Jerusalem Cinematheque hosts a film festival every July, with world cinema as well as New Israeli cinema on the program. ◈ 11 Hebron Rd., Jerusalem; 2 Sprintzak, Tel Aviv • Map N6 • (02) 565 4330, (03) 606 0800 • www.jer-cin.org.il

Jerusalem Cinematheque

Top 10 Israeli Artists and Writers

1 Chaim Bialik (1873–1934)
Israel's national poet wrote in Hebrew, contributing hugely to the revival of the language.

2 S. Y. Agnon (1888–1970)
This Nobel Laureate's seminal work was *The Bridal Canopy*.

3 Reuven Rubin (1893–1974)
Extremely influential on the emerging art of pre-state Israel, Rubin is known for his bright and optimistic works.

4 Mordecai Ardon (1896–1992)
Ardon's monumental triptych *At the Gates of Jerusalem* is on view at the Israel Museum.

5 Nachum Gutman (1898–1980)
A pioneer of Israeli art, Gutman is known for his bold and earthy paintings.

6 Yitzhak Danziger (1916–77)
This sculptor is most remembered for his controversial work *Nimrod*.

7 Yehuda Amichai (1924–2000)
The ironic poetry of Amichai reflects his intimacy with Jerusalem. Read *Tourists* and *Jerusalem* to get a taste.

8 A. B. Yehoshua (b.1936)
Hailing from Haifa, Yehoshua is best known for his book *The Lover*.

9 Amos Oz (b.1939)
Though bleak and intense, Oz's works are also illuminating. Read *The Hill of Evil Counsel*.

10 Daniel Barenboim (b.1942)
One of the world's finest conductors, Barenboim is a fascinating figure who has been accused of anti-Semitism by the ultra-right.

Left **Armenian ceramics** Center **Hebron glass** Right **Cosmetics made from Dead Sea minerals**

🔟 Things to Buy

1 Armenian Ceramics
Decorative pottery can be seen everywhere in the Old City. Traditional designs include intricate floral motifs, birds, and deer, all painted in characteristic cobalt blue, yellow, and green, on a white background. Some items can be custom-made, and nameplates make popular gifts.

2 Judaica
Finely crafted religious articles such as *mezuzahs* (prayer containers hung by doors), *menorah* (candlesticks), and *shofar* (the horn blown during Rosh ha-Shanah) make good souvenirs. The Cardo, in the Jewish Quarter, is a great place to shop for high-quality Judaica.

Antique teapot

3 Black-and-White Photos
Fascinating and affordable, photos of the Old City make lovely mementos. The most popular images are of Damascus Gate. Prints are available at some shops in the Old City souks.

4 Olive-Wood Objects
The craft of chiseling olive wood has been practiced in Bethlehem for centuries, and plays an important economic role for Palestinian Christians. Many beautiful olive-wood items are on sale here, including Christmas ornaments. ⓢ *Bethlehem* • *Map F4*

5 Antiques
Authentic antiques come with an export certificate so that you can legally take them out of the country. A few reputable shops deal in archaeological findings, such as terra-cotta amphorae, stone statues, and ancient glassware. Coins, earthenware pots, and oil lamps are more common.

6 Cosmetics
Some beauty products are unique to this region. Minerals from the Dead Sea are used in creams and soap, most famously by the Ahava company. The city of Nablus is synonymous with olive-oil soap, produced here for centuries. ⓢ *Ahava Store: The Cardo, Jewish Quarter* • *Map P4*

7 Hebron Glass
Hand-blown in Hebron since the 14th century, these attractive souvenirs are often made from recycled glass. Traditionally dark blue, turquoise, deep red, and green, the glass now comes in

Olive-wood souvenirs, Bethlehem

many hues. Baubles and amulets make good gifts, but you can even get a full dinner service. ❧ *Best bought in one of Hebron's factory showrooms, N of City Center • Map G4*

Books
Well-stocked bookshops offer translations of Hebrew and Arabic classics, or books about the political situation. The Steimatsky chain has English language sections, while The Bookshop at the American Colony Hotel in East Jerusalem is a landmark shop. However, books are relatively expensive here. ❧ *Steimatsky: 9 Mamilla Av. & 33 Jaffa Rd. • The Bookshop: American Colony Hotel: 1 Louis Vincent St., off Nablus Rd., Sheikh Jarrah, East Jerusalem*

Pickled condiments, Old City souk, Jerusalem

Local Delicacies
Bags of nuts, trays of olives, sticky dates, olive oil, towers of spices, and assorted dried fruits abound in both Arab and Israeli markets. Far tastier than the equivalent back home, they keep well and are easy to transport.

Bedouin Textiles
Vivid bedouin rugs, cushions, and textiles woven from camel hair or coarse wool are a great buy, particularly in Sinai. Finely embroidered items made in Palestinian workshops, including dresses, purses, and bags, are also very popular. ❧ *http://fansina.net*

Top 10 Places to Shop in Jerusalem

1 Sunbula
Buy jewelry, embroidery, rugs, soaps, toys, and trinkets here. ❧ *7 Nablus St., East Jerusalem • (02) 672 1707*

2 Palestinian Pottery
The most authentic place to buy hand-painted ceramics. ❧ *14 Nablus St., East Jerusalem • (02) 628 2826*

3 Jerusalem House of Quality
Artisans' workshops selling everything from pottery and jewelry to Judaica. ❧ *12 Hebron Rd. • (02) 671 7430*

4 Old City Souk
Head here for an amazing variety of souvenirs. Don't forget to haggle. ❧ *Old City*

5 Barakat Antiquarian
Unusually beautiful items, usually in an Oriental style, are on offer here. ❧ *American Colony Hotel • (02) 627 9723*

6 Mahane Yehuda
Stock up on spices, nuts, and local delicacies at this famous Israeli souk *(see p59)*.

7 Bezalel Market
A weekly street market selling jewelry, art, clothes, and accessories. ❧ *Bezalel Alley and Shatz St., West Jerusalem • Open 10am–4pm Fri*

8 Elia's Photo Service
This fixed-price shop is the best place to buy old prints. ❧ *14 Souq al-Khanqah, Christian Quarter • (02) 628 2074*

9 Educational Bookshop
Stocks mostly regional titles. There's also a café with Wi-Fi. ❧ *19 Saladin St., East Jerusalem • (02) 627 5858*

10 Baidun
Three adjacent shops selling antiquities, such as Roman glass and Hellenic statues. ❧ *28 Via Dolorosa, Old City • (02) 626 1469*

Israel, Sinai & Petra's Top 10

Left **Eid el-Adha** Center **Easter** Right **Blowing the** *shofar*, **Rosh ha-Shanah**

TOP 10 Religious Holidays and Festivals

1 New Year
Rosh ha-Shanah, the Jewish New Year, falls in September and marks the start of ten days of prayer. For Muslims, New Year begins on the first day of *Muharram*, which will be November 4 in 2013. January 1 is not a public holiday in Israel.

2 Purim
This festival falls between late February and early March and celebrates the deliverance of the Jews from genocide in ancient Persia. The events, told in the Book of Esther, are recited publicly from scrolls. An annual Purim parade is held in Tel Aviv.

Purim parade in Tel Aviv

3 Passover (Pesach)
In spring, Passover, or Pesach, remembers the liberation of the Jews from captivity, and their Exodus from Egypt. During Passover, Jews eat symbolic foods, including *matzah* (unleavened bread). The festival goes on for a week and the first and last days are official public holidays.

4 Easter
Celebrated on different dates by the Eastern and Western churches, Easter is a movable feast. On Good Friday and Easter Sunday, the crowds on the Via Dolorosa are a sight to behold. But most fervent is the Greek Orthodox celebration of Holy Saturday in the Church of the Holy Sepulchre *(see p9)*.

5 Eid el-Fitr
Lasting three days, the Muslim festival of Eid el-Fitr marks the end of Ramadan, the month of fasting. It is celebrated with special communal prayers, giving new clothes and gifts to children, and spending time with family. During Ramadan, devout Muslims fast from dawn till dusk. In 2013, Ramadan is speculated to last from July 9 to August 8.

6 Yom Kippur
The holiest time of the year for Jews, Yom Kippur is the Day of Atonement. Even non-practicing Jews fast for 25 hours, while the observant spend much of the day at the synagogue. The festival marks the end of 10 days of penitence that began on Rosh ha-Shanah. In 2013, it begins at sunset on September 13.

7 Sukkoth
From late September to early October, the Tabernacles festival sees Jews build makeshift *sukkah* (shelters) to commemorate the 40 years spent in the wilderness

after the Exodus. Meals are eaten there, and Orthodox Jews even sleep inside. Plywood and thatch booths can be seen in gardens, restaurants, and hotel receptions, and on balconies and rooftops.

Jews building a *sukkah*

Eid el-Adha
The most important Muslim festival, Eid el-Adha commemorates Ibrahim's (Abraham's) willingness to sacrifice his son to God. It also marks the end of the *Haj* (pilgrimage) to Mecca. The four-day celebration involves special prayers, the slaughter of sheep, feasts, charitable donation, and wearing new clothes. In 2013, it falls on October 15.

Hanukkah
The Jewish Festival of Lights commemorates the re-consecration of the Temple in 164 BC, and lasts eight days. Each day, families light a single candle in an eight-branched *menorah* (candlestick). It is the best time to be in Israel, when the streets are brightly lit. In 2013, Hanukkah will be from November 27 to December 5.

Christmas
During the Christmas period major centers of Christianity have religious processions, and there are special services in churches. The fairs, festivities, and decorations make it an attractive religious spectacle (see p21).

Top 10 Religious Faiths

1 Judaism
The first great revealed religion, Judaism instructs via the Torah, and the oral laws of the Mishnah and Talmud.

2 Samaritans
A dissident sect of Judaism, Samaritans live either in Nablus or Holon and now number just over 700.

3 Karaites
A sub-sect of Judaism dating back to the 8th century, Karaites believe that only the written Torah is binding. About 40,000 live in Israel.

4 Orthodox Christianity
Greeks are the dominant Orthodox group in Jerusalem. The Russians and Armenians also have a strong presence.

5 Catholicism
The Latin church arrived in Jerusalem with the Crusaders.

6 Islam
Founded by the Prophet Mohammad, Islam's armies conquered the Holy Land four years after his death in 636 AD.

7 Druze
This faith split from Islam in the 11th century, and has a central tenet of the "oneness of God." About 110,000 Druze live in Israel.

8 Circassian
This ethnic group migrated to Palestine in 1880 from the Caucasus in Central Asia. They are Sunni Muslims and live in two villages in the Galilee.

9 Ahmadiyyat
A revivalist sect of Islam founded in 1889, they believe that the Messiah has come in the person of Mirza Ghulam Ahmad.

10 Baha'i
The adherents of this faith, founded in 1844, believe all religions are essentially the same. The body of the Bab is enshrined in Haifa.

AROUND THE REGION

ISRAEL, SINAI & PETRA'S TOP 10

Left **Damascus gate** Center **Statue of David, Tower of David Museum** Right **Signage, Lions' Gate**

Jerusalem

THIS UNIQUE CITY *is sacred to the three great monotheistic faiths. Crammed with churches, mosques, synagogues, museums, and archaeological sites, the Old City has a chaotic exoticism that simply takes the breath away. Palestinian East Jerusalem contains fascinating sights and good nightlife, while to the west, the Jewish city encompasses excellent museums, markets, and restaurants. Jerusalem's 3,000-year history has been turbulent, to say the least. From 1949–1967, the city was divided along the Green Line, with the Jordanians controlling the east, including the Old City. The 1967 war saw Israel take control of the entire city. The mix of cultures and religions that jostle against each other in Jerusalem's streets leaves an impression that lasts a lifetime.*

Golgotha

The Dome of the Rock with the city in the background

Sights

1. Walls and Gates
2. The Citadel
3. Western Wall
4. Israel Museum
5. Church of the Holy Sepulchre
6. Haram esh-Sharif
7. Old City Souks
8. Jerusalem Archaeological Park
9. Mount of Olives
10. Mount Zion

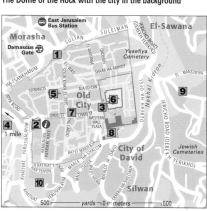

Preceding pages **The spectacular Baha'i Gardens, Haifa**

Walls and Gates

Seven gates, dating mostly from the time of Suleyman the Magnificent, penetrate the walls. Jaffa Gate was L-shaped to slow down attackers. The most impressive is Damascus Gate, which has crenellated battlements above, and the remains of the original gate and plaza, the start of the Roman Cardo, below. There are charming lion emblems on each side of Lions' Gate. The smallest is Dung Gate, close to the Western Wall, while Zion Gate is bullet-scarred from 1948. The Old City Ramparts Walk *(see p36)* is an enjoyable activity, affording astonishing views in all directions. ◈ *Map P4 • Ramparts Walk: open 9am–5pm Sat–Thu (till 4pm winter), 9am–2pm Fri; Adm (only the southern ramparts are open on Fri)*

The Citadel

Just within the city walls, the Citadel makes an arresting sight. The area was first fortified by Herod the Great in the 1st century AD, and has been destroyed and rebuilt many times. The present structure is largely medieval. Over the ages, the Citadel was occupied by various conquering forces. Inside, besides a museum on Jerusalem's history, there are viewpoints, a courtyard garden, and occasional art exhibitions *(see pp12–13)*.

Faithful at the Western Wall

Western Wall

This is the holiest site in Judaism, called "HaKotel" in Hebrew: worshippers come day and night and non-Jews can also insert prayers into the wall. The huge stone blocks were part of the retaining wall of the Temple Mount, not the Temple itself. A tour goes through the eerie Western Wall Tunnel, underneath the Muslim Quarter. It leads down a Herodian street alongside the wall, to emerge on the Via Dolorosa. ◈ *Western Wall Plaza • Map P4 • (02) 627 1333; 1 599 515 888 • Western Wall Plaza: open 24/7 • Western Wall Tunnel: open 8:30am–eve Sun–Thu, 8:30am–noon Fri; Adm; by guided tour only • www.thekotel.org*

Israel Museum

This museum, first opened in 1965, houses a magnificent collection of archaeology, artifacts, art, and design. Renovations have doubled the gallery space, and ensured that the presentation of objects is to the highest possible standard. Take time to wander the Billy Rose Art Garden, which offers a peaceful interlude among famous works of sculpture *(see pp14–17)*.

Phasael's Tower, The Citadel

Carry a bottle with you which you can fill up at the little water fountains around town.

Quarters of the Old City

Since medieval times, the Old City has been divided into quarters. The Muslim Quarter is the most populous and least explored. The Jewish Quarter, damaged during the Jordanian occupation, is largely rebuilt, and the Christian Quarter is awash with pilgrim hospices. Smallest is the Armenian Quarter, with 2,000 residents living behind high walls.

5 Church of the Holy Sepulchre

Seek out this most important of churches, tucked away in the Christian Quarter amid a warren of souvenir shops and crowded by other structures. To the right of the doorway, steps lead up to the domed Chapels of the Franks. This was the Crusader's ceremonial entrance to Golgotha, sealed by the Muslims after they re-took Jerusalem in 1187. The last five Stations of the Cross are within the church. Four of these are in Golgotha, while the last is, of course, Jesus's tomb itself *(see pp8–9)*.

6 Haram esh-Sharif

Meaning "Noble Sanctuary," this platform is also called Temple Mount. Tradition holds that this was where Abraham offered his son as a sacrifice to God. On top sits the Dome of the Rock, and other Islamic structures, including *sabils*. Previously, it was the site of the Jewish Temple and the Holy of Holies. Non-Muslims can only enter through the Moors' Gate, but can exit through any of the nine functioning gates *(see pp10–11)*.

7 Old City Souks

The most instantaneously captivating area of Jerusalem, the souks offer a mix of the exotic and the mundane. David Street, leading down from Jaffa Gate, is lined with souvenirs shops selling everything from Israeli army caps, Armenian pottery, and Nativity scenes to Palestinian *kaffiyahs*. A metal staircase leads to the rooftops and extraordinary views. Chain Street is a continuation of David Street, where souvenir stalls merge into fabulous Mameluke buildings. ✆ Map P4

8 Jerusalem Archaeological Park

This site reveals Jerusalem's history, from the First Temple period to the Umayyad era. Begin at the Davidson Center, which displays findings. Key remains include the vestiges of Robinson's Arch, a Herodian shopping street, a medieval tower, and Umayyad palaces. The flight of stairs on the south side once led up to the Second Temple. At the bottom of the steps are *mikvehs* (ritual baths), where pilgrims first purified themselves. ✆ *Inside Dung Gate • Map P5 • (02) 627 7550 • Open 8am–5pm Sun–Thu, 8am–2pm Fri • Adm • www.archpark.org.il*

Old City souk

Basilica of the Agony

9 Mount of Olives

This hill rises over the eastern edge of the Old City. From afar, most eye-catching are the golden domes of the Church of St. Mary Magdalene, built in the Muscovite style. Below this, the gilded mosaics on the Basilica of the Agony sparkle in the sun. Hidden within the trees are other churches associated with the last events of Jesus's life. The vast Jewish Cemeteries spread over the slopes of the mount are the oldest graveyards in the world (see pp18–19).

10 Mount Zion

Apart from the obvious biblical associations, Mount Zion is also linked with several important Christian events. A Crusader-era hall is believed to be where Christ and his disciples shared the Last Supper. The Tomb of David is located directly below. Dominating Mount Zion are the turreted conical dome and tall bell tower of the Dormition Abbey, venerated as the place where the Virgin Mary fell into "eternal sleep."

◉ Map N5 • Dormition Abbey: open 8:30am–noon & 12:30–5:30pm Mon–Sat, 10:30–11:45am & 12:15–5:30pm Sun
• Hall of the Last Supper: open 9am–5pm

Via Dolorosa (Way of Sorrows)

Morning

🕐 Millions believe that this was the last path Jesus walked, on the way to his crucifixion. From where he was condemned to where he was crucified, Stations of the Cross mark each event. Start at Lions' Gate and check out the acoustics in **St. Anne's Church** (see p38). A little way ahead is the First Station, outside Al-Omariyya Boys School. Opposite, the **Monastery of the Flagellation** (see p38) is the Second Station. Keep walking, under the Ecce Homo Arch, to the T-junction with El-Wad St. The Third Station is on your left, and to the right is the **Austrian Hospice** café (see p60). Stop here for a coffee. The Fourth Station is at the Armenian Church. Have lunch at **Abu Shukri** (see p43), slightly further on to the left.

Afternoon

Turn right and find the Fifth Station and the ascent to Golgotha. Shortly after the Sixth Station, **Baidun** shops (see p49) are worth a visit. The Via Dolorosa meets souk Khan el-Zeit, where you'll find the Seventh Station, and a short way up El-Khankah St. is the Eighth. Return to El-Zeit, turn right, and right again, and continue along to the doorway of the **Ethiopian Monastery** (see p9), where the Ninth Station is marked by a Roman pillar. Steps lead through the chapel to the Parvis in front of the **Church of the Holy Sepulchre** (see pp8–9). The final five Stations are inside.

Left **Convent of the Sisters of Zion** Center **Valley of Jehoshaphat** Right **Lady Tunshuq's Palace**

TOP 10 Sights In & By the Old City Walls

1 Muristan
Originally the site of an 8th-century pilgrim hospice, Muristan is now geared toward tourism. The Church of St. John the Baptist is one of the city's oldest churches, and close by, the Lutheran Church of the Redeemer offers awesome views from its bell tower. 🔊 Map P4

2 The Cardo
In Byzantine times, this was the main thoroughfare of the city. Excavations and reconstructions have turned it into an exclusive shopping arcade. 🔊 Map P4

3 Hurva Square
This square is dominated by the rebuilt Neo-Byzantine Hurva Synagogue. An adjacent minaret is all that is left of the 14th-century Mosque of Sidna Omar. 🔊 Map P5

4 City of David
Settled by the Canaanites in 2000 BC, this ridge is the oldest area in Jerusalem. King David supposedly took it for his capital about 1,000 years later. Don't miss the tour of Hezekiah's Tunnel (see p36). 🔊 Maalot Ir David • Map Q5

5 Garden Tomb
In the 19th century, General Gordon of Khartoum erroneously declared this hillock to be the site of Golgotha. Nonetheless, the garden is pleasant, and there is an ancient tomb here. 🔊 Conrad Schick St., East Jerusalem • Map P3

6 Lady Tunshuq's Palace
The Mamelukes' distinctive *ablaq* technique – using bands of alternate colored stone – is apparent in Lady Tunshuq's Palace. The three soaring doorways are inlaid with marble, and there is stalactite decoration on the windows. 🔊 El-Takiya St. • Map P4

7 Convent of the Sisters of Zion
Situated below Ecce Homo Arch, this convent contains the Struthion Pool and the flagstone "*lithostrothon*." 🔊 Via Dolorosa • Map P3 • (02) 627 7292

8 Valley of Jehoshaphat
This valley, where the dead will be resurrected on the Day of Judgment, contains the so-called Tomb of Zechariah, with a pyramid roof, and the conically roofed Absalom's Tomb. 🔊 Map Q4

9 Zedekiah's Cave
It is believed that Zedekiah escaped from the Babylonians in 586 BC via this massive cave. Herod also quarried it for building materials. 🔊 Map P3 • (02) 627 7550

10 Rockefeller Museum
Housed in a Neo-Gothic building, the museum displays Crusader-era marble lintels from the Church of the Holy Sepulchre, 8th-century beams from El-Aqsa, and stucco figurines from Hisham's Palace in Jericho (see p64). 🔊 27 Sultan Suleiman St. • Map Q3 • (02) 628 2251

Left **Ethiopia Street** Center **Vendors at Mahane Yehuda** Right **Russian Compound**

🔟 Sights in West Jerusalem

1 Yemin Moshe
This is a small area of delightfully renovated flower-filled lanes. Its highlight is Mishkenot Shaananim, which was built as a communal housing block but now functions as a guesthouse for artists. ✎ *Map N5*

2 Mahane Yehuda and Nakhlaot
For over 100 years Mahane Yehuda has been a buzzing market, and now its restaurant scene is burgeoning too. Nearby, the alleys of Nakhlaot are worth exploring. ✎ *Off Agrippas St. • Map L2*

3 Nakhalat Shiva
This old neighborhood has great bars and restaurants, plus lovely arty shops along its main alleyway. To the north lie Zion Square and Ben Yehuda Street – full of cafés and college kids. ✎ *Map M3*

4 Russian Compound
Built for Russian pilgrims in the 1860s, this enclosure's huge edifices include Sergei's Courtyard, the Holy Trinity Church, and a half-quarried monolithic column. ✎ *Map M3*

5 Mamilla
The 1949–67 armistice line ran through Mamilla. Many original buildings have been incorporated into the pedestrianized mall, which leases space to top international and Israeli brands. ✎ *Map M4*

6 Givat Ram
Called the "Museum Center," Givat Ram is home to the Knesset, the Supreme Court, the Botanical Gardens, and a campus of the Hebrew University. ✎ *Map J4*

7 Mea Shearim
An enclave of ultra-orthodox Jews, Mea Shearim resembles an 18th-century Polish ghetto. It was planned by German architect Conrad Schick (1822–1901). Ashkenazi food, black suits, and trails of children abound. ✎ *Map M2*

8 Ethiopia Street
This charming lane houses the circular Ethiopian church, designed by Conrad Schick. Other period buildings include a 19th-century Arab mansion at No. 6a. ✎ *Map M3*

9 The U. Nahon Museum of Italian Jewish Art
This museum contains a synagogue from Conegliano in the Veneto, complete with lavish gilded Baroque stucco. Also on display are silver Torah finials and illuminated manuscripts. Don't miss the ancient wooden Ark from Mantua (1543). ✎ *27 Hillel St. • Map M3 • (02) 624 1610*

10 German Colony
This attractive street has cafés, bars, and shops housed in Templar buildings and Arab villas. A farmers' market is held every Friday. ✎ *Emek Refaim St.*

Most of these sights are a short walk from the Old City.

Left **Jerusalem Hotel** Right **Rooftop bar at Mamilla Hotel**

ᵃⁿ10 Places to Drink

1 Jerusalem Hotel
Enjoy draught Taybeh in this crowded vine-covered courtyard. Middle Eastern and Western food is served. ⊗ *Nablus Rd., East Jerusalem • Map P1 • (02) 628 3282 • Open 8–10:30am & 11am–11pm*

2 Borderline
This expat haunt has a popular garden patio and is open till late. ⊗ *13 Sheikh Jarrah, East Jerusalem • Map P1 • (02) 532 8342 • Open noon–2am daily*

3 American Colony
Mingle with journalists, intellectuals, and artists over a drink here. The cave-like Cellar Bar is open all year. ⊗ *1 Louis Vincent St., off Nablus Rd., Sheikh Jarrah, East Jerusalem • Map P1 • (02) 627 9777 • Cellar Bar: open 6pm*

4 Mamilla Hotel
The rooftop bar at Mamilla has plush modern lounge-style seating, while Mirror Bar boasts chic lighting, a cocktail bar, and excellent DJs. ⊗ *11 King Solomon St., West Jerusalem • Map M5 • (02) 548 2222 • Rooftop: open 6pm–midnight Sun–Thu, noon–11pm Fri & Sat; Mirror Bar: open 8pm–late Sun–Thu, 9.30pm–late Sat*

5 Uganda
Near the Russian Compound, this super-cool bar serves Taybeh beer. There's live music or DJs every night. ⊗ *4 Aristobulus, West Jerusalem • Map M3 • (02) 623 6087 • Open noon–3am Sun–Fri, 2pm–3am Sat*

6 Austrian Hospice
Located in the Old City, this garden café is a real joy. A limited drinks menu keeps things simple. ⊗ *37 Via Dolorosa, Old City • Map P4 • (02) 626 5800 • Open 10am–10pm*

7 Casino de Paris
Well hidden in the Georgian Market in the souk, this bar is named after a Mandate-era British Officers' club. Great tapas are on offer. ⊗ *3 Mahane Yeduda St. • Map L2 • Open noon–late*

8 Bolinat
In the heart of the New City, this café-bar-restaurant serves light Italianesque salads and sandwiches. ⊗ *6 Dorot Rishonim, just off Zion Sq., West Jerusalem • Map M3 • (02) 624 9733 • Open 24 hrs weekly*

9 Barood Bar-Restaurant
Cozy Barood is great for a lone or sociable drink. Open on Shabbat, they have a huge variety of drinks, and excellent food, on offer. ⊗ *Feingold Courtyard, 31 Jaffa Rd. • Map M3 • (02) 625 9081 • Open 12:30pm–1am Mon–Sat*

10 Notre Dame Center Roof Top Wine & Cheese Restaurant
Indulge in a platter of Continental cheese while gazing at superb views from the roof of the Notre Dame Center. They have a fabulous wine list. ⊗ *3 HaTsanhanim, opposite New Gate • Map N4 • (02) 627 9177 • Open 5pm–1am Mon–Thu, noon–1am Fri–Sun*

Very few places in Israel are simply for drinking – all bars serve food as well.

Price Categories

For a three-course meal for one with half a bottle of wine (or equivalent meal), taxes and extra charges.

$	under $15
$$	$15–25
$$$	$25–40
$$$$	$40–55
$$$$$	over $55

Left **Lavan** Right **Arcadia**

🔟 Places to Eat

1 Cavalier
A mainly meat and seafood French menu, with Mediterranean touches, is Cavalier's specialty. ✪ *1 Ben Sira St., Nakhalat Shiva • Map M4 • (02) 624 2945 • Open noon–3:30pm & 6:30–11:30pm daily • $$$$*

2 Machne Yuda
Fresh meat, fish, and vegetarian dishes are complemented by a great cocktail and wine list. ✪ *10 Beit Yaakov, Mahane Yehuda • Map K2 • (02) 533 3442 • Open 12:30–4pm & 6:30–11:30pm Sun–Thu, two sittings: 11:30am & 1:30pm Fri, 7pm–11:30pm Sat • $$$$*

3 Arcadia
This courtyard restaurant uses fresh produce from Mahane Yehuda and herbs from its own garden. ✪ *10 Agrippas St. • Map L3 • (02) 624 9138 • Open evenings • $$$$$*

4 Arabesque
The Middle Eastern and international menu is decent, but patrons come here for the atmosphere. ✪ *American Colony Hotel • Map P1 • Open 11.30am–6pm & 7–10:30pm • $$$–$$$$$*

5 Askadinya
Situated within an Ottoman mansion, Askadinya offers perfect Middle Eastern cuisine, plus creative international dishes. ✪ *11 Sheikh Jarrah, East Jerusalem • Map P1 • (02) 532 4590 • Call ahead for opening times • $$$–$$$$*

6 Chakra
Try a selection of dishes for a reasonable price at Chakra. Do book in advance. ✪ *41 King George St. • Map L4 • (02) 625 2733 • Open 6pm weekly, from 12:30pm Sat • $$$–$$$$*

7 Tmol Shilsom
A cute dairy café, Tmol Shilsom serves comfort food. ✪ *5 Yoel Salomon St., Nakhalat Shiva • Map M3 • (02) 623 2758 • Open 9–1am Sun–Thu, 9am–1:30pm Fri • $$$*

8 Mona
High quality Mediterranean cuisine. Seafood, meat, and vegetarian dishes mix unusual flavors. ✪ *Artists' House, 12 Schmuel Hanagid St. • Map L4 • (02) 622 2283 • Open 5pm–2am Sun–Thu, noon–2am Fri & Sat • $$$$*

9 Te'enim
Creative vegetarian and vegan food, including tofu skewers, Tom Yam soup, salads, and bakes. Great views. ✪ *Confederate House, 12 Emil Botta, Yemin Moshe • Map M5 • (02) 625 1967 • Open 10am–10:30pm Sun–Thu, 10am–2pm Fri • $$$–$$$$*

10 Lavan
Light dairy meals include a good Italian selection. Lavan means "white," and the Scandinavian-style decor fits the bill. ✪ *11 Hebron Rd., in the Cinematheque • Map G4 • (02) 673 7393 • Open 10am–midnight • $$$$*

Left **Mosaic floor, Church of the Nativity** Center **Jericho** Right **Church of the Visitation, Ein Kerem**

Around Jerusalem

*S*EVERAL FULL- OR HALF-DAY EXCURSIONS *can be made from Jerusalem. Destinations to the west are in Israeli territory; those to the north and east are in the West Bank. Travel between the two is relatively simple. Remote monastic communities located in stunning settings in the southern Judaean Hills are worth a visit, while the northern hills are speckled with pale stone walls and olive orchards. Here, Nablus exudes charm while Ramallah is a lively city for nightlife. Near Bethlehem, Herodion offers one of Israel's most impressive vistas, and the oasis city of Jericho has a sultry vibe all its own.*

Italianate frescoes, Church of the Visitation, Ein Kerem

Ramallah, West Bank

Sights

1. Ein Kerem
2. Abu Ghosh
3. Bet Guvrin-Maresha National Park
4. Bethlehem
5. Hebron
6. Herodion
7. Jericho
8. Wadi Qelt
9. Ramallah
10. Nablus

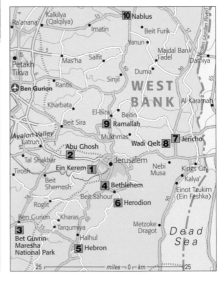

The village of Ein Kerem

Ein Kerem

Tradition holds that Ein Kerem was the home of John the Baptist. Important churches commemorating John's life dot the picturesque village, but the most striking of them all is the Russian Monastery with its golden onion-domes. Artisans' studios are sprinkled around the village and the surrounding hills make for pleasant walking. Ein Kerem is the perfect place to visit on Shabbat, as the churches remain open. ◈ *4 miles (7 km) W of Jerusalem • Map F4 • Light Rail, then Egged bus 28 from Har Herzl*

Abu Ghosh

This Arab village makes a nice excursion from Jerusalem. The Crusaders believed it to be Emmaus, where Christ appeared after his resurrection, and so the Knights Hospitallers built a Romanesque church here in the 12th century – it still stands, almost unchanged. On top of the hill is the Church of Notre Dame de l'Arche de l'Alliance, built in 1924 over a Byzantine church. Vocal music concerts are held in the churches biannually during Sukkoth and Shavuot. ◈ *8 miles (13 km) W of Jerusalem • Map F4 • Superbus 185 from Jerusalem • Crusader Church: open 8:30–11am & 2:30–7pm Mon–Wed, Fri & Sun; Notre Dame de l'Arche de l'Alliance: open 8:30–11:30am & 2:30–5pm*

Bet Guvrin-Maresha National Park

This undulating park is riddled by a network of caves. Quarried since Phoenician times, small surface holes reveal spiraling staircases, water cisterns, burial chambers, and columbaria. The ancient Judaean city of Tel Maresha is little more than a mound, but the burial caves of its Sidonian citizens have painted friezes of hunters and musicians. The apse of the Crusader Church of St. Anne makes a striking sight, while the Bell Caves are carved with Christian and Arabic inscriptions. The remains of a Roman amphitheater can be viewed opposite the park entrance. ◈ *Off Route 35, SW of Jerusalem • Map G3 • www.parks.org.il*

Bethlehem

Revered as the birthplace of Jesus, the imposing Church of the Nativity in Manger Square is the most important sight in Bethlehem. An attractive Franciscan church designed by Barluzzi, and a Greek Orthodox site with Byzantine remains are other attractions. The village center, with its narrow lanes, exudes an old-world charm *(see pp20–21)*. It is also worth making the short journey to the village of Beit Sahour, where the Shepherds' Fields are located.

Grotto of the Nativity

Traveling in the West Bank

Although tourists are never a target, it is wise to check the security situation on arrival. Getting around on Arab buses and service taxis is easy. The West Bank Barrier is easily visible, even if you drive around it rather than cross at a checkpoint. Many operators offer Palestinian tours.

Hebron

Political tension is ever-present in this populous town, which is divided between an Arab majority and hardcore Jewish settlers. Most areas are controlled by the Palestinian Authority and international peacekeepers. Others are patrolled by the Israeli military. The Cave of Machpelah, known as the Ibrahimi Mosque to Muslims, is split between the two religions *(see p66)*. The Arab markets and old souk offer some respite; buy the famed Hebron glass here. ◈ *25 miles (40 km) S of Jerusalem, West Bank • Map G4 • Egged bus 160 from Jerusalem*

Mosaic, Hisham's Palace

Herodion

A magnificent sight, this hilltop palace is named after Herod the Great. Ruins of bathhouses, towers, and mosaics dating from his time are tucked within the site. The summit affords amazing

Ruins at Herodion

views, and below lie pools and gardens from Herod's day, plus churches added by Byzantine rulers. Herod's tomb has also been discovered here after many years of searching. ◈ *Route 356, 7 miles (11 km) SE of Bethlehem, West Bank • Map F4 • Taxi from Bethlehem • Open summer: 8am–5pm Sat–Thu, 8am–3pm Fri; winter: 8am–4pm Sat–Thu*

Jericho

Settled 10,000 years ago, Jericho is reputedly the world's oldest city. The book of Joshua describes how the Israelites brought down Jericho's walls with a trumpet blast, and excavations at Tel Jericho have uncovered the remains of 7,000-year old walls and a stone tower. A cable car connects the Tel to the Monastery of the Temptation on the cliff face *(see p66)*. Hisham's Palace, built in AD 724, lies in ruins, but retains its mosaic floors. ◈ *25 miles (40 km) E of Jerusalem, West Bank • Map F5 • Arab bus 36 to Al-Azariyya, then change to service taxi • Tel Jericho & Hisham's Palace: Open summer: 8am–6pm Sat–Thu, 8am–5pm Fri; winter: 8am–5pm Sat–Thu, 8am–4pm Fri • Adm*

Wadi Qelt

This stunning 17-mile (28-km) long ravine is located between Jerusalem and Jericho. A path runs along its full length. Lined with palm trees and green foliage, it contrasts sharply with the arid hills. A Herodian aqueduct also follows the course of the stream. The hike passes St. George's Monastery *(see p66)* and continues to Jericho. The Roman road

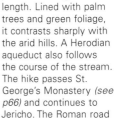

Carry your passport at all times when traveling in the West Bank.

running along the top of Wadi Qelt gorge is accessible by car and leads to the car park near the monastery. ◉ *Signed off Route 1 • Map F5*

A busy produce market in Ramallah

9 Ramallah

This city at the heart of Palestine has oodles of atmosphere. Al-Manarah Square is the commercial center, chock-full of vendors, shoppers, and noise. The Old City retains its Ottoman charm, and the mausoleum of Yassar Arafat in Al-Bireh is worth a visit. Weina Ramallah Festival, held in July, is a window into Palestinian culture. Ramallah is also known for its nightspots.
◉ *10 miles (16 km) N of Jerusalem, West Bank • Map F4 • Arab bus 18 from Damascus Gate • Tourist Information Center: Issa Ziadeh St.; (02) 296 3215 ext 414; Open 9am–5pm Sat–Thu*

10 Nablus

A maze of authentic markets, cobbled streets with arches, and crumbling mansions, Nablus offers an alternative to modern life. It is the site of Joseph's Tomb, and so the area remains a political hot spot. An Ottoman clock tower, Turkish *hamams* (bathhouses), and Roman amphitheaters are dotted around the town. The Samaritans *(see p51)* live nearby on Mount Gerizim.
◉ *N of Jerusalem, West Bank • Map E4 • Arab bus 18 to Ramallah, then service taxi*

A Walk in Ein Kerem

Afternoon

🕐 After lunch, take the Light Rail to Har Herzl. Disembark, follow the sign to Yad Vashem down a side road, but turn immediately left into the forest, where a stony track descends through a wooded valley. This agreeable walk finishes at the rear of the **Church of St. John the Baptist** *(see p66)*, less than 30 minutes later. The church opens at 2:30pm, so if you are

☕ early, have coffee at one of several hole-in-the-wall cafés. After visiting, cross the main road and follow the sign to Mary's Spring, which is topped by a quaint mosque. From here, steps ascend to the right, to the **Church of the Visitation** *(see p66)*. Admire the split-level church and great vista, and then retrace your steps. Before the main road, turn left and follow the sign to painter Yitzhak Greenfield's studio to see his Jerusalem-inspired work. Continue to the Notre Dame de Sion Guesthouse (closed on Sunday) and ring the bell to enter. You can visit the church and cemetery, and sit a while in the peaceful garden, which has wonderful views across the valley to the golden roof of the Russian Monastery. The lane loops back to the main road. There is no shortage of restaurants and café-bars to choose from, but a fail-safe option

🍴 for dining is **Karma** *(see p67)*, which has plenty of window seating. Afterwards, enjoy a streetside beer at **Mala Bar** *(see p67)*, where there is outdoor heating on chilly evenings.

If hiring a car, make sure the insurance covers driving in the West Bank.

65

Left **Nebi Musa** Center **Church of the Visitation** Right **Mar Saba Monastery**

Top 10 Holy Places Around Jerusalem

1 Church of St. John the Baptist
Dating from the 17th century, this Franciscan church was built over the ruins of Byzantine and Crusader structures. Steps lead down to the Grotto of St. John. ⊗ *Ein Kerem • Map F4*

2 Church of the Visitation
Designed by Barluzzi, this two-tiered church commemorates Mary's visit to the mother of John the Baptist. ⊗ *Ein Kerem • Map F4*

3 Bethany
This tranquil cluster of buildings marks where Jesus is believed to have raised Lazarus from the dead. There's a Franciscan church, Lazarus' Tomb, a silver-domed Greek church and even a mosque here. ⊗ *Al-Azariyya village, E of Jerusalem • Map R5*

4 Church of the Nativity
Palestinian militants took refuge inside this church in Bethlehem in 2002, starting a 39-day long siege *(see p20)*.

5 St. George's Monastery
This 5th-century Greek monastery is hewn into the side of a stunning gorge. ⊗ *Off Route 1, 17 miles (27 km) E of Jerusalem, Judean Hills • Map F5*

6 Nebi Musa
Sultan Baybars built a shrine to Moses here in 1269. The cenotaph has since come to be revered by Muslims as Moses' tomb. ⊗ *Off Route 1, 6 miles (10 km) S of Jericho, Judean Hills • Map F5*

7 Mar Saba Monastery
This remote desert retreat was founded in AD 482 by St. Saba. His remains are said to be under a canopy inside the church. ⊗ *Off Route 398, 11 miles (17 km) E of Bethlehem, Judean Hills • Map F5*

8 Monastery of the Temptation
This cliff-side Greek monastery was built around the grotto where the Devil tempted Jesus. ⊗ *1 mile (2 km) N of Tel Jericho • Map F5*

9 Monastery of St. Gerasimos
This complex was founded by St. Gerasimos in the 5th century. Nearby, Qasr al-Yehud claims to be where John baptized Jesus. ⊗ *Route 90, SE of Jericho • Map F5*

10 Cave of Machpelah/ Ibrahimi Mosque
This is the second holiest site in the land for both Muslims and Jews. The Tomb of the Patriarchs is split in two – into a synagogue and a mosque. ⊗ *Hebron, 25 miles (40 km) S of Jerusalem • Map G4*

Entrance to all holy sites is free.

Price Categories

For a three-course meal for one with half a bottle of wine (or equivalent meal), taxes, and extra charges	**$** under $15
	$$ $15–25
	$$$ $25–40
	$$$$ $40–55
	$$$$$ over $55

Left **Afteem** Right **Azure**

🔟 Places to Eat

1 Zaitouneh Restaurant
Located within an Arabesque hotel, the Jacir Palace, this stylish restaurant is known for Lebanese food, but there are also many Italian choices. ✎ *Jerusalem-Hebron Rd., Bethlehem • Map F4 • (02) 276 6777 • Open noon–4pm & 6–11pm • $$$*

2 Dar al-Balad
Located in a restored old house in the center of Beit Sahour, Dar al-Balad serves Oriental dishes and salads. ✎ *Main St., Beit Sahour, Bethlehem • Map F4 • (02) 274 4007 • Open 10am–11pm • $$*

3 Afteem
Close to the Church of the Nativity, Afteem is the best place for falafel. ✎ *Manger Sq., Bethlehem • Map F4 • Open 8am–late Mon–Sat • $*

4 Azure
This old converted villa has a smart restaurant, a large bar, and a popular garden-patio. Their burgers are legendary, but the menu also includes Asian and Arabic food. Cocktails available. ✎ *Al Ma'ahed St., Ramallah • Map F4 • (02) 295 7850 • Open 11am–midnight daily • $$$*

5 Pronto's Resto-bar
You'll find the best pizza in town in this cozy trattoria. Warm-colored walls are adorned with artifacts and the front patio is a great spot for a draught Taybeh. ✎ *Al-Rahsheed St., Ramallah • Map F4 • (02) 289 7312 • Open 8am–midnight • $$$*

6 Ziryab
This spacious café serves tasty Eastern and Western food, as well as alcohol. There's also free Wi-Fi. ✎ *Salah Building, Rakob (Main) St., Ramallah • (02) 295 9093 • Open 11am–late daily • $$$*

7 Mala Bar
Pasta and salads are served at this cute candle lit restaurant-bar, which has tables along the village's main street. There are heaters in winter and a tiny, cozy indoor space to huddle up in. ✎ *Ein Kerem St., Ein Kerem • Map F4 • (02) 642 2120 • Open 6pm–late Mon–Fri, from noon–late Sat & Sun*

8 Karma
The extensive menu at this split-level restaurant is hearty and portions are absolutely huge. ✎ *74 Ein Kerem St., Ein Kerem • Map F4 • (02) 643 6643 • Open 10am–midnight Sun–Wed, 10am–1am Thu–Sat • $$$*

9 Lebanese Food Restaurant
This restaurant is heaven for hummus-lovers. If you have any room left after the *meze*, main dishes include Middle Eastern grills. ✎ *88 HaShalom St., Abu Ghosh • Map F4 • (02) 570 2397 • Open 9am–11pm • $$*

10 Majda
Run by an Arab-Jewish couple, Majda mixes local cooking with New Israeli Cuisine. ✎ *Ein Rafa, off Route 1, opposite Abu Ghosh • Map F4 • (02) 579 7108 • Open Wed–Sat • $$$$*

Left **Lutheran church, American-German Colony** Center **Neve Tzedek** Right **Eretz Israel Museum**

Tel Aviv

FOUNDED IN 1909 BY 66 FAMILIES, *Tel Aviv (Hill of the Spring)* has come far in little over a century. This city is the modern face of Israel, where contemporary thought, cuisine, nightlife, and culture are centered. Designed as a garden city by Sir Patrick Geddes in 1925, it is characterized by lovely parks, palm trees, and wide boulevards. Countless cafés and restaurant-bars line sunny streets, and the clean Mediterranean beach adds to the holiday atmosphere. The city saw a great population explosion during 1920–25. Later, when Jews arrived from the Bauhaus School in Germany, they began constructing in the International Style, creating 4,000 buildings within two decades – the highest concentration in the world. This legacy was recognized in 2003, when UNESCO declared the "White City" a World Heritage Site.

Holidaymakers kayaking and sailing in the Mediterranean

Sights

1. Beachfront Promenade
2. Jaffa
3. Bialik Street
4. American-German Colony
5. Neve Tzedek
6. Old Port
7. Yemenite Quarter
8. Rothschild Boulevard
9. HaYarkon Park
10. Ramat Aviv

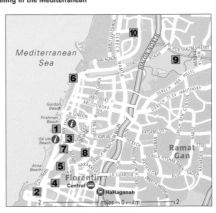

Beachfront Promenade

This is where the youthful soul of Tel Aviv lies. Stretching across the length of the city, the white-sand beach is crowded with people all summer long, sunbathing and playing *matkot* (see p44). Weekends are mayhem, especially after dark when the beachfront bars start buzzing. The southern end offers the best surfing, but swimmers should take note of the flag system – there are strong currents here. ◎ *Map U2*

Jaffa

Ancient Jaffa *(see pp22–3)* still feels exotically Middle Eastern, despite much renovation in recent times. The Visitors' Center in Kedumin Square shows a short film about the history of the area. Since the 1960s, the heart of the old town has been developed as an Artists' Quarter, with alleys that are named after the signs of the zodiac. The Ilana Goor Museum is also here, with a shop selling the artist's bronze statuettes. Ajami is an Arab district extending from Jaffa's southern end, with Ottoman-era architecture and a dilapidated charm. ◎ *Map T6 • Ilana Goor Museum: 4 Mazal Dagim; (03) 683 7676; Open 10am–4pm Sun–Fri, 10m–6pm Sat • Most businesses in Jaffa stay open on Shabbat*

Beit Ha'ir and Felicja Blumental Music Center

Bialik Street

Many historic buildings line this peaceful street. Beit Ha'ir, the old town hall, is now a museum telling Tel Aviv's history. The eye-catching saffron building next door is the Felicja Blumental Music Center. Opposite, the Design Museum of the International School has furniture and pieces of European Bauhaus design. The house of Chaim Bialik *(see p47)* has been restored with original furnishings and decor. A few doors down, the Reuven Rubin Museum has a display of his paintings, and a preserved studio. ◎ *Map V3 • Beit Ha'ir: 27 Bialik St.; (03) 724 0311; Open 9am–5pm Mon–Thu, 10am–2pm Fri & Sat; www.beithair.org*

American-German Colony

In 1866, American Messianic Christians from Maine set up a farming community here, doomed to fail as the climate bore no resemblance to that of their homeland. German Templars moved in and built the Lutheran Church in 1904; stained-glass windows were added in the 1970s. The Maine Friendship House, brought from the US and re-erected here, is open to visitors, while the Beit Immanuel Guesthouse has fine views from the roof. ◎ *Map U5*

Old Jaffa

Manshiye

Founded in 1888 as the first Arab quarter outside Jaffa, Manshiye disintegrated after the 1949 war, when residents fled and buildings were destroyed. The minaret of the Hassan Bek Mosque was used by snipers during the war. The Etzel Museum gives more information on the battle for Jaffa.

5 Neve Tzedek

Built in the 1880s as the first Jewish neighborhood outside Jaffa, Neve Tzedek is a desirable locale, with flower-filled lanes, boutiques, and nice places to dine. Its focal point is the Suzanne Dellal Centre (see p47), which hosts dance, theater, and music events. Close by, a museum dedicated to Nachum Gutman (see p47) displays his paintings of the new city. The house of the Rokach family is on the same street, while at Lilienblum Street the facade of the Eden Cinema, active from 1914–74, remains intact. ◈ Map U4 • Gutman Museum of Art: 21 Shimon Rockach St.; (03) 516 1970; Open 10am–4pm Sun–Thu, 10am–2pm Fri (free), 10am–3pm Sat • Adm

6 Old Port

The revived and redesigned port (namal) has rolling sweeps of wooden decking and exudes a truly Mediterranean vibe. Diverse restaurants, cafés, and shops line the boardwalk. Great for families during the day, the port is the perfect place for an evening drink, and later a busy nightlife spot. In Hangar 12, an eco-building powered by green energy, there is a farmers' market that sells organic goods. ◈ Map E3 • Farmers' Market: Open 8am–8pm Mon–Sat • www.namal.co.il

7 Yemenite Quarter

Bang in the city center, the Yemenite Quarter is a warren of tiny streets of low-rise, shabby-chic houses, peppered with hole-in-the-wall eateries serving authentic food. This merges into the HaCarmel Market (see p73), the city's largest and liveliest bazaar. Pedestrianized Nakhalot Binyamin Street has eclectic buildings that blend Moorish, Classical, and Art Nouveau styles. On Tuesdays and Fridays it hosts an arts and crafts fair. ◈ Map U3

8 Rothschild Boulevard

One of the city's most prestigious addresses, this leafy street is lined with some fine Bauhaus architecture (see p72). Independence Hall, at No. 16, was the home of Meir Dizengoff, the city's first mayor, and where Ben-Gurion declared Israel's independence on May 14, 1948. At No. 23 is the three-level Haganah

Yachts and boats moored at the quay, Old Port, Tel Aviv

Museum, which documents the the origins of the IDF. There's free Wi-Fi all along Rothschild's central promenade, and lovely places to eat and drink. ✆ *Map W3* • *Independence Hall: (03) 517 3942; Open 9am–2pm Sun–Thu; Adm* • *Haganah Museum: (03) 560 8624; Open 8:30am–4pm Sun–Thu; Adm*

Rothschild Boulevard

HaYarkon Park

Lining the Yarkon River in north Tel Aviv, this pleasant park offers a good adventure playground for kids, plus a bird park and tropical garden. Row boats can be hired on the lake, and the Sportech complex has a climbing wall, basketball courts, and a skate park. On the northern edge are the Meymadion Water Park and the Luna Park fairground *(see p37)*. ✆ *Map E3*

Ramat Aviv

An upmarket suburb, Ramat Aviv is home to the Tel Aviv University, whose grounds house the excellent Beit Hatfutsot (Museum of the Jewish People) *(see p35)*. A succession of other interesting museums lie along the southern edge, including the Eretz Israel Museum and the Yitzhak Rabin Center *(see p35)*. Between these two sits the Palmach Museum, telling the story of the Jewish guerilla fighters who took on the British after World War II. ✆ *Map X1* • *Palmach Museum: 10 Chaim Levanon; (03) 643 6393; www.palmach.org.il*

A Day Down the Promenade

Morning

🕐 The 3½-miles (5.5-km) promenade is an enjoyable walk. Bring your towel and sunblock, and pick your favorite beach. First, try a refreshing organic juice at the farmers' market at the **Old Port**. Heading south, you'll pass walled Nordau Beach, segregated for Orthodox Jewish bathers. Next is the Hilton Beach, opposite Independence Park, which is lively and gay-friendly. The south side of the beach is one of the best spots for surfing. Continue to the marina, bobbing with small yachts, where anyone can use the famous Gordon Pool ($13–$19). Make a quick detour inland to No. 17 Ben-Gurion St. and check out Ben-Gurion House. Come back to Gordon Beach and have a coffee or a beer at the excellent Gordo Beachfront Café.

Afternoon

Further ahead, Fishman Beach attracts large crowds. Stick to the promenade until you reach the Hassan Bek Mosque in Manshiye. Tel Aviv's hippies congregate on the adjacent Dolphinarium Beach on Friday afternoons, for drumming sessions, Capoiera, and juggling. Charles Clore Park contains **Manta Ray** restaurant *(see p75)* by Alma Beach, and also the Etzel Museum. From here, head inland to trendy **HaTachana** *(see p23)* to browse the shops or try tapas at the Vicki Cristina wine bar. Head back to the promenade and you are virtually in **Jaffa** *(see pp22–3)*.

Share your travel recommendations on **traveldk.com**

Left **Rothschild Boulevard** Right **Bialik Street**

🔟 Bauhaus Buildings

1 9 Gordon Street
This block has asymmetrical balconies and a recessed left side. The concrete pergolas criss-crossing the roof are intended as sun-breakers. ✎ *Map V1*

2 Kikar Dizengoff
Some marvelously restored buildings grace this square. Cinema Hotel, built in 1939, is a good example of the International Style, with ribbons of horizontal windows, curbed balconies, and overhanging ledges. ✎ *Map V2*

3 14 Ben Ami Street
Now serving as the Kabbalah Center, this building has a large balcony shading the windows underneath. ✎ *Map V2*

4 Yael Street
Building No. 6 on this street has asymmetrical windows and balconies enclosed within a symmetrical frame. It is all horizontal planes in No. 5, save for the emphasized vertical of the stairwell, which provides natural light and air circulation. Note the porthole windows and tiles made in Germany. ✎ *Map W2*

5 12 Tel Hai Street
This building incorporates the boat-shape, conceptualized by Erich Mendelsohn, the first notable German-Jewish architect to arrive. He used curves to take the edge off the harshness of modern life, which was criticized as being contrary to Bauhaus. ✎ *Map W2*

6 Bialik Street
Bialik's House at No. 22 has some Bauhaus features, but with added Moorish touches. No. 18 has two balconied wings enclosing a central garden. Functional No. 21 is home to a Bauhaus design museum. ✎ *Map V3*

7 65 Sheinkin Street
Built in 1935, the Rabinsky House uses practical fixtures to create decorative elements. The balconies are horizontal, with holes to allow the breeze to cool the building. ✎ *Map V3*

8 Ahad Ha'am Street
No. 49 creates a series of semicircles and painfully angled balconies. No. 57 is Cubist, with a few tiny windows. Nos. 93, 95, and 126 have typical horizontal strips of window. ✎ *Map V4*

9 Rothschild Boulevard
A perfect white cube sits at No. 71, with unbalanced windows and slit balconies. The Rubinsky House at No. 82 has a characteristic vertical glass stairwell. No. 142 has curved projecting balconies with balustrades, a flat roof, and cafés at ground level *(see p70)*.

10 Maze Street
No. 41 was the first structure to be built on stilts in Tel Aviv. No. 56 sits in front of the Diaghilev Hotel, a late-20th-century block that echoes the structure of the original 1934 building. ✎ *Map W4*

The Bauhaus School was driven by socialist ideals, and is characterized by basic functional forms and shapes.

Left **Flea market** Center **Artists' Quarter** Right **A designer boutique in HaTachana**

🔟 Shopping Areas

1 Sheinkin Street
Upmarket Sheinkin used to be the hub of Tel Aviv's Bohemian fashion scene. Sidewalk cafés, and independent boutiques and eateries still give the chain stores a run for their money. ◈ *Map V3*

2 Shabazi Street
Fashion designers, jewelers, ceramicists, and shoe boutiques abound along this street. Great for a spot of window-shopping. ◈ *Neve Tzedek • Map U4*

3 Azrieli Centre
These triangular, square, and circular space-age skyscrapers define Tel Aviv's skyline. There's a three-level shopping mall inside, and an observatory deck on the 49th floor of the round tower. ◈ *Map X2 • Adm to the observatory*

4 Gan HaHashmal
Don't be discouraged by the seedy look; this is where to buy cutting-edge fashion, jewelry, and footwear. ◈ *Map W4*

5 HaTachana
Housed in the restored old Jaffa train station, this is a self-contained complex of designer boutiques, handmade jewelry, and a couple of great eating options *(see p23)*.

6 Dizengoff Street
This is Tel Aviv's main retail street. The Bauhaus Center at No. 99 is an essential stop for gifts, and Kikar Dizengoff has a flea market every Tuesday and Friday. Dizengoff Center mall is at the southern end. ◈ *Map V2*

7 HaCarmel Market
The fresh produce section at this traditional souk is legendary, and side alleys specialize in spices, fish, nuts, and sausages. ◈ *Map V3 • Open 8am–5pm Sun–Fri*

8 Nachalot Binyamin
On Tuesday and Friday, this buzzing pedestrianized street hosts an arts and crafts fair. Glassware, jewelry, and Judaica are available. ◈ *Map V4 • Open 9:30am–5:30pm Tue, 9am–4pm Fri*

9 Artists' Quarter, Jaffa
The lanes here are crammed with studios and galleries. Buy original works by the sculptress in the Ilana Goor Museum, or check out Israeli poster art at the Farkash Galley *(see pp22–3)*.

10 Flea Market, Jaffa
Spread across the sidewalk or stacked onto stalls, genuine antiques vie with utter rubbish in this flea market, while vintage shops and quaint cafés mingle in *(see pp22–3)*.

Left **Bar at The Container** Right **Shalvata**

🔟 Bars and Nightlife Spots

1 Yoezer's
A sophisticated wine bar in a unique vaulted Ottoman building. The French-inspired food is excellent. ◈ *2 Yoezer Aish Habira, near the clock tower, Jaffa • Map T6 • (03) 683 9115 • Open 12:30pm–1am Sun–Thu, 11–1am Fri & Sat*

2 The Container
This "project space" mixes live music shows and art with food and alcohol. Located in one of the converted warehouses on the port, it's very popular with cool Tel Avivians. ◈ *Warehouse 2, Jaffa Port • Map S6 • (03) 683 6321 • Open noon–late Sun–Thu, 10am–late Fri & Sat*

3 Abraxas
This trendy two-level lounge-bar has a relaxed atmosphere. There's a pool table, and live DJs, and the food is good, too. ◈ *40 Lilienblum St. • Map V4 • (03) 510 4435 • Open 12pm–4am Mon–Thu, 1pm–4am Fri & Sat, 6pm–4am Sun*

4 Lima Lima
A dance/lounge bar hosting theme nights, of which Notorious GAY on a Monday is the most famed. ◈ *42 Lilienblum St. • Map V4 • (03) 560 0924 • Open 9:30pm–6am daily*

5 HaMaoz
Choose between the large front patios, a cool square bar in the center, or the apartment-style back room. There is also a pool table. ◈ *32 HaMelekh George St. • Map V3 • (03) 620 9458 • Open 8pm–3am Sun–Thu, 2pm–3am Fri, 6pm–late Sat*

6 Porter & Sons
This place serves great food and has 50 beers on tap. The styling is British, and it's hugely popular with Israelis. ◈ *14 HaAarba • Map X3 • (03) 624 4355 • Open noon*

7 Mike's Place
With a young vibe, cheap drinks, an international crowd, and a great beach location, Mike's Place is convenient and fun. Tex-Mex and Italian food is available. ◈ *86 Herbert Samuel • Map U2 • (03) 510 6392 • Open 11am–late*

8 The Minzar
This characterful bar is cheap and a bit grungy, but it is one of the best hangouts in the city to meet people. Excellent bar food and lots of drinks. ◈ *60 Allenby St. • Map V3 • (03) 517 3015 • Open 24/7, closed Yom Kippur*

9 Shalvata
A collection of bars linked by seating, the rooftop bar in summer is the best. Great sea views, and there's also an Italian-Mediterranean menu if you get peckish. ◈ *Tel Aviv Port • (03) 544 1279 • Open 5pm Mon–Thu, 9am Fri & Sat, closed Shabbat*

10 Radio EPGB
For a slightly alternative, underground, hip night out, this place is recommended for its music. Different DJs every night. ◈ *7 Shadal St. • Map W4 • (03) 560 3636 • Open 9pm–7am Mon–Sun*

Practically every bar in Israel also serves food.

Price Categories

For a three-course meal for one with half a bottle of wine (or equivalent meal), taxes, and extra charges

$	under $15
$$	$15–25
$$$	$25–40
$$$$	$40–55
$$$$$	over $55

Left **Fresh salad at Herbert Samuel** Right **Catit**

🔟 Restaurants

1 Catit
One of Israel's flagship restaurants, Catit offers haute cuisine with a great value lunch deal. ✆ *14 Haihal Hatalmud St., Neve Tzedek • Map V4 • (03) 510 7001 • Open noon–3pm & 7–11pm • $$$$–$$$$$*

2 The Dining Hall
A trendy restaurant, hugely popular with locals and tourists alike. ✆ *TAPAC, 23 Shaul HaMelekh Blvd. • Map X2 • (03) 696 6188 • Open noon midnight • $$–$$$*

3 Herbert Samuel
This stylish restaurant uses the freshest local ingredients in its Mediterranean-feel dishes. ✆ *6 Kaufman St. • Map T4 • (03) 516 6516 • Open 12:30–4pm & 6pm–midnight Wed–Sat • $$$$–$$$$$*

4 Haj Khalil
With authentic Arabic cuisine, this handy restaurant by the clock tower is the perfect place for a break from sightseeing. ✆ *18 Raziel St., Jaffa • Map T5 • (03) 518 8866 • Open 11am–midnight Sat–Thu, 11am–1am Fri • $$$*

5 Raphael
The lunch deals here include a spread of *salatim*, taking in Mediterranean, fish, and seafood flavors. ✆ *87 HaYarkon St., King David Tower • Map U3 • (03) 522 6464 • Open noon–4pm & 7–11pm daily • $$$$–$$$$$*

6 Orna & Ella's
A popular café-style place with a long-standing menu, perfect location, and modern Italian dishes. ✆ *33 Sheinkin St. • Map V3 • (03) 620 4753 • Open 8:30am–midnight Sun–Thu, 10am–midnight Fri & Sat • $$$*

7 Brasserie
This Art Deco restaurant-bar has a French slant. ✆ *70 Ibn Gvirol • Map W1 • (03) 696 7111 • Open 24 hrs • $$$–$$$$*

8 Mul Yam
The use of international ingredients and the unique wine list are ground-breaking. ✆ *Hanagar 24, Tel Aviv Port • (03) 546 920 • Open 12:30–3:30pm & 7:30–11pm Sun–Fri, 1–4pm & 9:30–11pm Sat • $$$$–$$$$$*

9 Thai House
Run by a Thai-Israeli couple, this place has a relaxed vibe and attracts a young crowd. Courses from the Isan region of Thailand are on offer. ✆ *8 Bograshov St. • Map V2 • (03) 517 8568 • Open noon–11pm • $$$*

10 Manta Ray
Located at the southern end of the promenade, Manta Ray uses fresh local ingredients and is famed for its Mediterranean fish. ✆ *Alma Beach • Map T5 • (03) 517 4773 • Open 9am–midnight daily • $$$$*

Unless otherwise stated, all restaurants accept credit cards and serve vegetarian meals.

Left **Cana** Center **The village of Majdal Shams** Right **Ruins of a Roman colonnade, Beth Shean**

Galilee and the North

THIS IS ISRAEL'S GREENEST REGION, *with lush valleys and wooded hills. Brimming with wildflowers in spring and crisscrossed by hiking trails, it is a good place for horse-riding, bird-watching, and other outdoor activities. The sparkling Sea of Galilee is a major draw, where Tiberias makes a good base for exploring sites central to Jesus's ministry. The region is also steeped in Jewish religious history. The town of Safed has winding streets and ancient synagogues that captivate visitors, while the region's wealth of archaeological sites – Caesarea, Beth Shean, and Tsipori – is overwhelming. A visit to Akko is like stepping back in time, and nearby Haifa is bright and bustling. The Golan Heights, a popular weekend retreat, has some excellent wineries.*

Sea of Galilee

Akko

🔟 Sights

1. Haifa
2. Akko
3. Nazareth
4. Cana (Kafr Kana)
5. Tiberias
6. Sea of Galilee
7. Upper Golan
8. Lower Golan
9. Safed (Tzfat)
10. Harod Valley

Baha'i Shrine and Gardens, Haifa

Haifa

1 The centerpiece of this sea-side city is the Baha'i Gardens, containing the golden Shrine of the Bab. In the German Colony, Ben-Gurion Street is lined with attractive Templar buildings, many of which have been turned into restaurants, bars, or hotels. Haifa has a mixed population, and the lanes of the Arab area of Wadi Nisnas contain great local eateries. Carmel district has some quality restaurants, while the port is becoming popular for its nightlife. Museum buffs will be spoilt for choice, as the city boasts excellent Japanese art, science, modern art, maritime, and naval history museums. ◈ *Map C3 • Tourist Office: 48 Ben-Gurion St.*

Akko

2 This picturesque Arab town (the historic Acre) has an authentic old city enclosed by solid walls. Several mosques, a citadel, the lively souk, Turkish *khans* and a *hamam* are all 18th-century structures built on top of a subterranean Crusader city. The beautiful Baha'i Gardens outside Akko's walls rival Haifa's and are equally sacred as they contain the Tomb of the Prophet Baha'u'llah. Akko also has great fish restaurants by its colorful harbor, and one of the most famous hummus joints in Israel *(see p43).* ◈ *Map B4 • Visitors' Center, Festival Garden • 1 700 7080201 • Most sites open 8:30am–5pm daily (till 4pm Fri) • Adm*

Nazareth

3 Most of Nazareth's sights are within the old Arab town, which centers on the confusing maze of the souk. Famous as Jesus's childhood home, the town has many churches, but the Basilica of the Annunciation *(see p39)* dominates with its modern dome. The Greek Orthodox St. Gabriel's church is a delight, and hidden in the alleyways are the Synagogue church and the Mensa Christi church, interspersed with Ottoman mansions and great restaurants. ◈ *Map C4*

Cana (Kafr Kana)

4 Tradition holds that Jesus turned water into wine in this large Arab village near Nazareth. Two churches compete to commemorate the event. The Franciscan church has an ancient mosaic and crypt, but the Greek church is prettier and contains stone jars which were allegedly involved in the miracle itself. ◈ *Map C5 • Churches St. • Franciscan Church of the Wedding Feast: open 8am–noon & 2–6pm Mon–Sat; Greek Orthodox Wedding Church: open 8am–3pm Mon–Sat, closed Sun afternoon • 5 miles (8 km) NE of Nazareth*

Greek Orthodox Wedding Church, Cana

Greek Orthodox Church at Capernaum

Christ's Ministry
Jesus of Nazareth did much of his preaching by the shores of the Sea of Galilee. This is where he walked on water, fed the 5,000, gave the Sermon on the Mount, and expelled a legion of devils.

Tiberias

This large and lively resort town was founded in Roman times to utilize the nearby hot springs. These still remain an attraction, along with several popular beaches. Roman ruins at Hammat Tiberias National Park include a zodiac mosaic in the synagogue. One of four Jewish holy cities, Tiberias has tombs of many eminent rabbis, which attract worshippers. Old mosques join Catholic, Greek, and Protestant churches on the water's edge. ◈ *Map C5 • Tourist Office: 23 HaBanim St.; (04) 672 5666*

Sea of Galilee

Israelis call this lake the Kinneret, and it's a scenic holiday spot. Important Christian sites dot the banks. At Tabgha, a church marks the supposed site of the Feeding of the Five Thousand. Capernaum has archaeological remains, including a synagogue, Roman houses, and a church built over the house of the apostle Peter. Uphill from Tabgha, the Mount of Beatitudes has an octagonal church and sublime views. At Yardenet, on the south side of the lake, white-gowned pilgrims gather to be baptized in the Jordan River. ◈ *Map C5*

Upper Golan

Captured from Syria in 1967, the Golan is known for stunning scenery and dramatic viewpoints. The peak of Mount Hermon has skiing in winter *(see p45)*, while Nimrud Castle is a superbly located Mameluke fortress. The walks, waterfalls, and archeological sites at Banias National Park are fun for all ages. Boutique industries flourish in *moshavim* and kibbutzim in the area while Druze towns and villages, such as Majdal Shams and Masada, make for a strong contrast and have their own local dishes. ◈ *Map A6 • Adm for Nimrud Castle, Banias National Park, and Mount Hermon • www.parks.org.il*

Lower Golan

A good region for getting immersed in the outdoors: some of Israel's best hiking is in the Yehudia Nature Reserve. The Zavitan Canyon leads to hexagonal pools, while Yehudia Canyon entails swimming through pools of icy water. Katsrin, the regional capital, was founded in 1977. There's an ancient Jewish settlement and an archaeological museum here, and

Sea of Galilee

The Mediterranean coast is lined with beautiful beaches, all the way from Tel Aviv to Nahariya in the north.

the visitors' center shows a 3D film about the area. Gamla National Park has walking trails. 🚶 *Map B6 • www.parks.org.il*

Safed (Tzfat)
9 Jews have been drawn to this city since their expulsion from Spain during the Christian Reconquest, and it is a center of Kabbalic mysticism. Medieval synagogues remain active places of worship, while the former Arab quarter is now an Artists' Colony. The Beit HaMeiri Museum is also worth a visit. At Mount Meiron, 6 miles (9 km) northwest, the Tomb of Shimon sees festivities on the eve of Lag BaOmer. 🚶 *Map B5*
• *Synagogues: Open 9:30am–5pm Sun–Thu (till noon Fri); Beit HaMeiri Museum: 8am–2:30pm Sun–Thu (till 1:30pm Fri)*

Synagogue, Safed

Harod Valley
10 This valley is edged to the south by the Gilboa mountain range, which has a scenic driving route, walking trails, and viewpoints. Ruins of the Roman city of Beth Shean *(see p80)* at the valley's eastern end are the most extensive in the country. The turquoise pools at Gan HaShlosha National Park are perfect for bathing, while close by, the Beth Alpha synagogue *(see p80)* has a well-preserved mosaic floor. There's an art museum and a lovely café in the Ein Harod kibbutz. 🚶 *Map C5*
• *Kavim buses 411 and 412 to Beth Shean*

Around the Sea of Galilee

Morning

🕐 Start early with the majestic view from the Horns of Hattin (off Route 72, W of Tiberias), where Saladin's armies defeated the Crusaders. Then treat yourself to a great-value breakfast at Shavit's Guesthouse in Moshav Arbel. Stop at Kibbutz Ginosar and check out the 2,000-year-old fishing boat in the museum. Proceed to the Christian sites of Tabgha, the Mount of Beatitudes, and Capernaum. The ancient Jewish town of **Korazim** *(see p80)* is further up the hill. At the northern point of Galilee, you can ride inner tubes down the river at the Jordan River Park, or save getting wet for the water-slides at **Luna Gal Water Park** *(see p37)* on Route 92. Otherwise, just relax on one of several nice beaches on this eastern shore. Pause awhile at Kursi's ancient church, a small site with pretty mosaic floors.

Afternoon

Kibbutz Ein Gev is a good place for a spot of lunch, either at **Marinado Banamal** *(see p81)*, or the nearby Ein Gev Fish Restaurant. Continue south, then make a detour 5 miles (8 km) southeast along Route 98 for a soak at the hot springs in Hamat Gader. There is also a crocodile farm here, and it is worth spending as much time there as possible. Finish off the day with a wander around the resort town of **Tiberias** and a leisurely drink at one of its waterfront bars.

Left **Waterfall at Banias** Center **Nimrud Castle** Right **Mona Lisa of the Galilee**

TOP 10 Archaeological Sites

1 Belvoir Castle

This fortress evokes images of the siege by Saladin's armies in 1191, which eventually forced the Crusaders to surrender.
⊘ Off Route 90, 17 miles (27 km) S of Tiberias • Map C5 • (04) 658 1766

2 Beth Shean

Israel's best-preserved Roman city has remains dating back as far as the Canaanite era.
⊘ Map D5 • (04) 658 7189

3 Beth Alpha

This 6th-century synagogue has an almost intact mosaic floor showing the Ark of the Covenant and a central zodiac design.
⊘ 7 miles (11 km) W of Beth Shean • Map D5 • (04) 653 2004

4 Megiddo

According to the Book of Revelation, Armageddon will take place here. Dating from approximately 7000 BC, Megiddo has been excavated four times and many layers of ruins have been unearthed. ⊘ Route 66, 22 miles (35 km) SE of Haifa • Map C4 • (04) 659 0316

5 Tsipori

The ancient town of Tsipori is famous for its mosaics. The most famous among them is the "Mona Lisa of the Galilee."
⊘ Route 79, 2 miles (3 km) NW of Nazareth • Map C4 • (04) 645 4768

6 Caesarea

Herod the Great built this port city and named it after Augustus Caesar. There are remains of Byzantine streets, a Crusader citadel, and palaces.
⊘ Off Rd. 2 • Map C3 • (04) 626 7080

7 Gamla

In AD 67, thousands of Jewish rebels held out for seven months under Roman siege here. The park's cliffs are home to nesting vultures and there are waterfalls to visit. ⊘ Route 808, Lower Golan • Map B6

8 Korazim

Remains of residences, ritual baths, dolmens, and a synagogue can be seen in this ancient Jewish town. ⊘ Route 8277, off Route 90, N of Tiberias • Map B5 • (04) 693 4982

9 Banias

This popular park has walking trails that lead past Ptolemaic, Roman, Crusader, and Islamic remains. ⊘ Off Route 99, 9 miles (15 km) E of Kiryat Shmona • Map A6 • (04) 690 2577

10 Nimrud Castle

Perched atop a narrow ridge, this castle was built by Muslim rulers in the 13th century. The walls and moat are well preserved, and the views unsurpassed. ⊘ NE of Banias • Map A6 • (04) 694 9277

→ *For details on all these sites, see www.parks.org.il.*

Price Categories

For a three-course	**$** under $15
meal for one with half	**$$** $15–25
a bottle of wine (or	**$$$** $25–40
equivalent meal), taxes	**$$$$** $40–55
and extra charges.	**$$$$$** over $55

Above **Al-Reda**

Places to Eat

1 Helena
Overlooking Caesarea's harbor, Helena has an excellent location. It serves top-notch Mediterranean food. ◈ *Old Harbor, Caesarea National Park • Map C3 • (04) 610 1018 • Open noon–11pm • $$$$$*

2 Diana
For over 30 years, Diana has been dishing up classic Middle Eastern cuisine. ◈ *Grand New Hotel, 5050 St., Nazareth • Map C4 • (04) 657 2919 • Open11am–midnight • $$$-$$$$*

3 Al-Reda
This restaurant is housed in an Arab mansion. The food is great for both vegetarians and meat eaters. ◈ *21 El-Bishara St., Nazareth • Map C4 • (04) 608 4404 • Open 1pm–2am Mon–Sat, 7pm–2am Sun • $$$$*

4 El Babur
This famed Arabic restaurant has two branches. Reservations are essential on weekends. ◈ *Ein Ibrahim Junction, Umm el-Fahm (on Rd. 65) • Map D4 • (04) 611 0691 • Open 10am–11pm daily • $$$-$$$$*

5 Uri Buri
This fish and seafood restaurant in an Ottoman mansion on Akko's shore is a magical place. Try the chef's tasting menu. ◈ *HaHagana St., Akko • Map B4 • (04) 955 2212 • Open noon–11pm daily • $$$*

6 Maayan Habira
This traditional Jewish pub has been a Haifa institution for over 50 years. It serves East European food, draught beers, and has a great atmosphere. ◈ *4 Natanzon St., Haifa • Map C3 • (04) 862 3193 • Open 8am–5pm Sun–Fri, 8am–midnight Tue • $$*

7 Fattoush
Choose between outdoor seating under citrus shrubs or the candlelit cavern at funky Fattoush. Oriental and international cuisine is offered. ◈ *38 Ben-Gurion, German Colony, Haifa • Map C3 • (04) 852 4930 • Open 9am–1am • $$$*

8 Nechalim
This restaurant serves French-and -Italian inspired cuisine and has some lovely riverside seating. Ingredients are locally sourced, and the menu is almost entirely meat and seafood. ◈ *Gan HaZafon Mall, Rd. 99, North Galilee • Map A6 • 04 690 4875 • Open noon–4pm & 6–11pm Fri, noon–11pm Sat & Sun • $$$-$$$$*

9 The Cauldron of the Witch and the Milkman
The specialties here are rich casseroles and dishes that use local ingredients. ◈ *Nahal Nimrod, Upper Golan • Map A6 • (04) 687 0049 • Open noon–9pm Sun & Sat • $$$$*

10 Marinado Banamal
Renowned for high quality steaks, lamb, and other meaty dishes, Marinado caters to vegetarians as well, and it's good for kids. ◈ *Kibbutz Ein Gev, Route 92, E side of the Sea of Galilee • Map C6 • (04) 665 8555 • Open 9am–late • $$$$*

Left **Ein Ovdat** Center **The formidable Makhtesh Ramon crater** Right **Ibex at Ein Gedi**

Dead Sea and the Negev

FAMOUS THE WORLD OVER *as the place where the Dead Sea Scrolls were discovered, this region is peppered with sites of biblical significance. The imposing rebel fortress at Masada lies to the southwest of the Dead Sea, while shoreline spa resorts tempt tourists with their therapeutic, mineral-rich mud treatments. Ein Gedi oasis is a particularly enticing emerald swath in the creamy hills. The vast crater of Makhtesh Ramon in the Negev Desert and the eerie beauty of the Wilderness of Zin are best seen while on a hike. Kibbutzim are turning the desert green again, as Ben-Gurion desired, and the bedouin are trying to find a balance between their traditional culture and modern life.*

People floating in the highly saline water of the Dead Sea

Ein Gedi hike

🔟 Sights

1. Qumran
2. Ein Gedi
3. Masada
4. Beersheva
5. Ein Ovdat
6. Ovdat
7. Makhtesh Ramon
8. Mitspe Ramon
9. Timna National Park
10. Eilat

The caves at Qumran

Qumran

In 1947, a bedouin shepherd looking for a lost goat stumbled into a cave full of jars containing the Dead Sea Scrolls. They had been hidden from the Romans 2,000 years ago by a desert community of ascetic Jews who awaited the Messiah, while living a life of ritual purity. The scrolls are on display in the Israel Museum *(see pp14–17)*, but at Qumran you can see an archaeological site, a museum, and a film. It is worth making the scramble up to the caves themselves, but allow at least two hours and take lots of water. ⊗ *Route 90, 12 miles (20 km) S of Jericho • Map F5 • (02) 994 2235 • Open 8am–5pm Sat–Thu, 8am–4pm Fri • Adm*

Ein Gedi

A spring-fed oasis, Ein Gedi is like a slice of the tropics in the middle of the desert. Attractions are spread over a few miles. Two gorges belonging to the Nakhal David and Nakhal Arugot rivers lie at the center of the Nature

Waterfall, Ein Gedi Nature Reserve

Reserve and ibex and rock hyrax are often sighted. A beach is located about a mile (1.6 km) south of the reserve. Kibbutz Ein Gedi, further south, has a fabulous botanical garden and hotel *(see p116)*. At the Ein Gedi Health Spa, you can try mud treatments and soak in sulfur pools. ⊗ *Route 90, 35 miles (56 km) S of Jericho • Map G5 • (08) 658 4285 • Open summer: 8am–5pm; winter: 8am–4pm • Adm • www.parks.org.il; www.ein-gedi.co.il*

Masada

This World Heritage Site towers over the western edge of the Dead Sea. During the Jewish Revolt of AD 66–73, almost 1,000 rebels killed themselves here rather than submit to the rule of Rome. After the Romans left, the site was apparently deserted for 200 years. However, in the 5th century, Christian hermits established a monastery here. The remains of a Byzantine church can still be seen *(see pp24–5)*.

Beersheva

Traditionally known as the place where Abraham purchased a well, this town was revived by the Ottomans, and some great architecture from their time remains. The former Governor's Residence, now the Negev Art Museum, and the mosque next door merit a special visit; pick up a map with a walking tour of Turkish buildings from the Visitors' Center. A bedouin market, held every Thursday, sells livestock, produce, and souvenirs. Tel Beersheva, a city dating from the 11th century BC, lies 4 miles (6 km) northeast. ⊗ *Map H3 • Visitors' Center: 1 Hebron Rd.; (08) 623 4613; Open 8am–4pm Sun–Thu, 8am–12pm Fri*

Floating in the Dead Sea
The high salt content in the water makes sinking impossible. But swimming is not feasible either – you simply bob on the surface. However, floating is a sensation like nothing else on Earth. Be sure not to splash water in your eyes, and be warned that skin abrasions sting agonizingly.

Ovdat

5 Ein Ovdat
One of Israel's most stunning walks is along the Nahal Zin gorge in this national park. The white-walled ravine has springs feeding ice-cold glassy pools. From the lower entrance, the walk passes a waterfall, a poplar grove, and rock-hewn steps before finishing with a clamber up metal ladders to the upper car park. Ibex are often seen on the escarpment. The grave of Ben-Gurion is located in Midrashet Sde Boker, next to the lower entrance. ◈ Route 40, 32 miles (52 km) S of Beersheva • Map A2 • (08) 655 5684 • Egged bus 392, Metropoline bus 60 • Open summer: 8am–5pm, winter: 8am–4pm • Adm • www.parks.org.il

6 Ovdat
This settlement was founded in the 3rd century BC by the Nabataeans, as a way station on the Spice Route. It sits on a hilltop overlooking desert canyons and an ancient network of irrigation canals. Many of the ruins here date from Byzantine times, including the remains of two churches and hundreds of cave dwellings. In 2005, Ovdat was declared a UNESCO World Heritage Site. ◈ Route 40 • Map A2 • (08) 655 1511 • Egged bus 392, Metropoline bus 60 from Beersheva • Open 8am–5pm (till 4pm Fri and winter) • Adm • www.parks.org.il

7 Makhtesh Ramon
Israel's version of the Grand Canyon, this is the largest erosion crater in the world, some 25 miles (40 km) long and 1,310 ft (400 m) deep. It is scattered with mountains and colorful rock formations, and laced with hiking and biking trails. Jeep tours, stargazing, and camping are also possible. In ancient times, the Nabataean spice road between Petra and Gaza crossed the crater. Before embarking on treks, buy proper maps. ◈ Route 40, 50 miles (80 km) S of Beersheva • Map B2 • Visitors' Center: (08) 658 8691; Open 8am–5pm Sat–Thu, 8am–4pm Fri • Adm

8 Mitspe Ramon
Perched over the rim of the Makhtesh Ramon, this little town makes a great base for exploring the crater. Founded in 1956, it is experiencing a cultural and culinary awakening. The industrial center has been revamped into the Spice Routes Quarter, with old hangars turned into boutique hotels, dance studios, restaurants, and shops. There are also

Views across Makhtesh Ramon

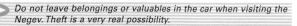

Do not leave belongings or valuables in the car when visiting the Negev. Theft is a very real possibility.

good budget places to stay in town. ❧ *Route 40, 15 miles (24 km) S of Ovdat • Map A2 • Egged bus 392, Metropoline bus 60 from Beersheva*

9 Timna National Park
This expanse of rocky desert contains archaeological remains, stunning rock formations, and the oldest known copper mines in the world. Ancient Egyptians mined here around 1500 BC, and left two temples dedicated to the goddess Hathor. Solomon's Pillars afford stunning views, while the Mushroom Rock is a favored photo stop. A re-creation of the Tabernacle carried by the Israelites during the Exodus can be visited at set times. Walking and driving trails link the sites.
❧ *Route 90, 18 miles (28 km) N of Eilat • Map B2 • (08) 631 6756 • Adm • www.timna-park.co.il*

A beach at Eilat as seen from the Red Sea

10 Eilat
A busy resort town on the Gulf of Aqaba, Eilat draws tourists with its nightlife, tax-free shopping, and year-round sun. Clear waters and colorful marine life in the Red Sea make diving and snorkeling worthwhile. Alternatively, the Coral World Underwater Observatory gives a close-up view of corals and fish, and also has tanks of sharks and turtles. Trips to Petra or Sinai are easily organized from Eilat.
❧ *Map C2 • www.coralworld.com/eilat*

Along the Dead Sea in a Day

Morning

🕐 After an early breakfast, leave Jerusalem via Route 1 and drive 25 miles (40 km) to join Route 90 at the north end of the Dead Sea. The first stop is the archaeological site and caves at **Qumran** *(see p83)*. A short way south, tackle the twisting road up to **Metzoke Dragot Viewpoint** *(see p86)*, to take some photos in the morning light. Back on Route 90, it's a 10-minute drive to the Ahava Factory, where you might pick up a good deal on mineral products. The oasis at **Ein Gedi** nature reserve *(see p83)* is about 6 miles (10 km) further south, offering walks, wildlife, and ancient ruins. Spend at least a couple of hours here. Have lunch at Pundak Ein Gedi, by the beach, or carry on to Kibbutz Ein Gedi to eat at the Botanical Gardens restaurant. In either case, the Botanical Gardens are worth visiting afterward.

Afternoon

From the gardens, either head toward the mountain-top fortress at **Masada** *(see pp24–5)* to explore the archaeological remains of Herod's stronghold, before heading to the beach at **Ein Bokek** *(see p86)* for a float and a cooling shower; or visit the Dead Sea first, saving Masada for the magical light at sunset (those making this trip in reverse may want to start with the classic Masada sunrise). There are refreshments at Masada, and an Aroma Café in Ein Bokek.

Left **Metzoke Dragot Viewpoint** Center **Einot Tzukim** Right **Mount Sodom**

Best of the Rest

Northern Beaches
These beaches have good restaurants. Basic rooms and camping facilities are available, or just pay for day-use of the loungers and towels. ✆ *Off Route 90, 1 mile (2 km) from Kalia Junction*

Einot Tzukim (Ein Feshka)
This park, with freshwater pools and streams, is a bright splash of green between the cliffs and the Dead Sea. There are some small archaeological remains from the Herodian Period. ✆ *Route 90 • Map F5*

Metzoke Dragot Viewpoint
A steep and snaking road (signed off the highway) leads up to the top of sheer cliffs. It finishes with views of the Dead Sea and mountains in Jordan that are breathtaking. ✆ *11 miles (17 km) S of Einot Tzukim • Map G5*

Ein Bokek
This is the main resort district on the Israeli edge of the Dead Sea. Fancy hotels all offer spa and mud treatments. The public beach has showers *(see p85)*.

Sodom
This starkly beautiful landscape is accessible only by tour or jeep. Mount Sodom, in-land, is composed almost entirely of salt and riddled with caves. The actual location of the biblical Sodom is more likely to be on the Jordanian side. ✆ *Route 90, 31 miles (50 km) S of Ein Gedi • Map H5*

Makhtesh HaGadol and HaKatan
These two erosion craters offer trekking, scattered ruins, and lovely vistas. Drive across the Makhtesh HaGadol, and to an observation point over the Makhtesh HaKatan that affords spellbinding views. ✆ *Map A2*

Mamshit
This is the best-preserved Nabataean city. The Negev Camel Ranch nearby has hourly camel treks which do not require pre-booking. ✆ *Route 25, 5 miles (8 km) S of Dimona • Map A2*

Arad
This town on a desert plateau has a small artists' quarter and good hiking. Tel Arad, 5 miles (8 km) away, was a major city in the Canaanite and Israelite periods. ✆ *Map H4*

Shivta and Nitzana
These remote Nabataean cities are romantic, rarely visited ruins. Shivta, dating from the 1st century BC, has impressive water systems and Byzantine churches. Nitzana lies close to the Egyptian border. ✆ *Map A2*

Khai Bar Yotvata Wildlife Reserve
This drive-through safari park breeds animals mentioned in the Bible and other near extinct species, including leopards, oryx, and raptors. ✆ *Route 90, 22 miles (35 km) N of Eilat • Map B2*

Price Categories

For a three-course	**$** under $15
meal for one with half	**$$** $15–25
a bottle of wine (or	**$$$** $25–40
equivalent meal), taxes,	**$$$$** $40–55
and extra charges	**$$$$$** over $55

Above **Patrons dining at Eddie's Hideaway**

☺10 Places to Eat

1 Yakota
This Moroccan restaurant offers salads, couscous, and *tagines*, as well as some unusual meat dishes. ☺ *27 Mordey Hagetaot, Beersheva • Map H3 • (08) 623 2689 • Open 11am–3pm Fri, 7pm–midnight Sat • $$$$*

2 Little India
This cheap and casual place has vegetarian and some fish dishes. The Israeli-Indian owner has added Jewish touches alongside the classic Indian fare. ☺ *15 Ringelblum St., Beersheva • Map H3 • (08) 648 9801 • Open 11am–11pm Sun–Thu, 11am–3pm Fri • $$*

3 Taj Mahal
Arabic and Western food is served here. With a poolside setting, and Oriental furnishings, it's the best dining spot in town. ☺ *Tulip Inn Hotel, Fin Bokek • Map H5 • 057 650 6502 • Open noon–2am • $$$*

4 Lalo
The home-cooked dishes include *tagines*, stuffed veg, and fish done the spicy Moroccan way. A great budget choice. ☺ *259 Horev St., Old Center, Eilat • Map C2 • (08) 633 0578 • Open 11:30am–5pm Sun–Thu • $$*

5 Beresheet Hotel
Great views of the Makhtesh and gourmet dishes in the Rosemary restaurant make dining here a memorable experience. ☺ *1 Beresheet Rd., Mitspe Ramon • Map A2 • (08) 659 8004 • Open 1pm–3pm & 6:30–8pm • $$$–$$$$*

6 Chez Eugene
Mediterranean cuisine with an emphasis on Negev produce is on the menu here. The Israeli wine list is excellent. ☺ *8 HarArdon, Spice Routes Quarter, Mitspe Ramon • Map A2 • (08) 653 9595 • Open 7–10pm • $$$$*

7 Pundak Ne'ot Smadar
A roadside inn with a delightful setting. There's a country-kitchen inside, and the organic meals use ingredients grown on the kibbutz. ☺ *Shizafon Junction, Neot Smadar • Map B2 • (08) 635 8180 • Call ahead for opening times • $$$*

8 The Last Refuge
High-quality seafood defines this restaurant. There's a vast menu and servings are generous. The Red Sea is just outside. ☺ *Almog Beach, Eilat • Map C2 • (08) 637 3627 • Open 12:30–11pm • $$$$*

9 Eddie's Hideaway
This homey restaurant has an old-fashioned menu, and a friendly owner. Renowned for the meat dishes, it is popular with locals, so do book in advance. ☺ *68 Almogim St. (off Elliot), Eilat • Map C2 • (08) 637 1137 • Open 6–11:30pm Sun–Fri, 2–11:30pm Sat • $$$–$$$$*

10 Soomsoom
This eatery, run by women from kibbutz Samar, serves wonderful organic veggie food. There's also a health food store. ☺ *Old Center • Map B2 • Open 9am–3pm Sun–Thu, 9am–2pm Fri • $$–$$$*

➤ *Unless otherwise stated, all restaurants accept credit cards and serve vegetarian meals.*

Left **Camel safari in Sinai** Right **Dahab**

Sinai Peninsula

THE IDYLLIC WHITE-SAND BEACHES *that stretch along the coast of the Gulf of Aqaba are Sinai's biggest tourist draw. The warm waters of the Red Sea contain a wealth of marine life and corals, enticing both experienced and novice divers. Sharm el-Sheikh is popular with families, couples, divers, and party-people alike, while independent travelers head north to the mellow and secluded beaches at Dahab, Nuweiba, and beyond. The region is also steeped in history. Pharaohs mined the land for turquoise and gold, and momentous Old Testament events occurred in the mountainous interior. Visit the fascinating St. Catherine's Monastery, take a jeep or camel safari to explore unspoiled oases, and trek through the craggy mountains of South Sinai.*

Colorful Red Sea corals

Nuweiba

 Sights

1. Sharm el-Sheikh
2. Ras Mohammad National Park
3. St. Catherine's Monastery
4. Mount Sinai
5. Dahab
6. Ras Abu Galum
7. Wadi Feiran
8. Nuweiba
9. The Colored Canyon and Ain Khudra
10. Taba and Surrounds

Preceding pages **The imposing fortress at Masada**

Nightlife at Sharm el-Sheikh

Sharm el-Sheikh
Egypt's "Red Sea Riviera" boasts year-round sun, diverse restaurants, lively nightlife, and good shopping. Naama Bay has a long beach lined with world-class hotels. Sharm el-Maiya, a few miles south, has a vibrant market and cheaper restaurants. The region is also a favored diving destination; the colorful reefs are superlative, and sharks and shipwrecks are commonplace. Bright corals and shoals of fish can be seen while snorkeling and on glass-bottom boat trips. Horse-riding, quad-biking, and golf are also available. Tours to St. Catherine's Monastery and desert safaris are offered by many travel agents. ✆ Map D2

Ras Mohammad National Park
This is one of the world's top diving spots and the warm waters are also perfect for snorkeling. The park has around 20 dive sites but Shark Reef, the most southerly, is the best for varied marine life. Huge varieties of coral create wonderful shapes, patrolled by hundreds of types of fish, including deep-water species. The coastal scenery is magical too, with mangroves, beaches, and dramatic cliffs. Note that entry to the park (by boat or land) requires a "full Egypt visa." ✆ 12½ miles (20 km) S of Sharm el-Sheikh • Map D2 • Adm

St. Catherine's Monastery
This fortified monastic retreat contains the Basilica of the Transfiguration, built in AD 527. Behind the iconostasis, you can see the exquisite Mosaic of the Transfiguration on the roof of the apse. The holiest part of the complex is the Chapel of the Burning Bush behind the apse, which is usually closed to the public. The monastery also holds a collection of thousands of manuscripts and icons *(see pp26–7)*.

Mount Sinai
Called *Jebel Musa* in Arabic, this mountain was where Moses received the Ten Commandments from God. Many pilgrims and groups climb up for views of the sunrise. Two routes ascend the 7,500-ft (2,286-m) peak. The most popular, the Camel Path, takes about 3 hours. Camels can be hired next to the Monastery, but the final 700 steps have to be climbed on foot. The 3,700 Steps of Repentance offer a shorter but tougher ascent. A chapel and a mosque are located at the summit. ✆ 56 miles (90 km) W of Dahab and Nuweiba • Map D1
• Compulsory to hire a camel or a guide

Climbing Mount Sinai

 Check the latest security situation before you travel to the Sinai Peninsula.

Divers at Dahab

Dahab

Sinai's independent traveler
scene centers on Dahab, which
means "gold" in Arabic. However,
for expanses of golden sand you
have to head north or south, since
in Dahab itself, the seashore is
almost entirely lined with beach
cafés. Although the old bedouin
village has been dwarfed by
commerce, the laidback atmosphere remains. Experienced
divers relish the challenge of the
canyon and the infamous Blue
Hole. Strong winds on this stretch
of coast make it a top spot for
wind- and- kite-surfing. ⊗ *Map D2*

Ras Abu Galum

Located within a designated
protectorate, the wild beach of
Ras Abu Galum is inhabited by
bedouin fishermen. Visitors come
here on camel or diving trips
organized in Dahab or Sharm.
The snorkeling is superb, with
aquamarine waters revealing a
host of marine life and a reef just

off the beach. About half a mile
to the north, the Blue Lagoon
has perhaps the most startling
turquoise sea and white-sand
beach in all Egypt. ⊗ *Map D2*

Wadi Feiran

This lush oasis presents a
shock of green among the jagged
orange mountains. A monastery,
dedicated to Moses, lies at the
southern point of the fertile
valley. Here, the tiny community
of Greek Orthodox nuns maintains
two churches and a guesthouse.
On an adjacent hillock are the
remains of the 4th-century
monastery, the oldest Christian
site in Sinai. About half a mile
(0.8 km) north, there are bedouin-
run campsites. Hikes and camel
safaris can be arranged from
here. Further north, a squat
bedouin village has some shops.
⊗ *34 miles (55 km) W of St. Catherine's
Monastery • Map C1 • Monastery: (069)
385 0071/2 • By taxi from St. Catherine's
Monastery • Open 9–11:45am Mon–Sat*

Nuweiba

The ferry from Aqaba docks
at Nuweiba's port. The city,
a short taxi ride away, has
restaurants and other
amenities. A range of
campsites and a
couple of hotels dot
the huge swath of
beach in between. To
the north, the bedouin
village of Tarabin has a
soft sandy beach with
snorkeling spots off
the end. The pink
mountains across the

Wadi Feiran

*A "full Egypt visa" is required to visit Sinai's west coast and Ras
Mohammad National Park. A "Sinai only" permit is not sufficient.*

sea in Saudi Arabia sparkle with lights at night. Despite being hit by the dip in Israeli tourism, plenty of new-age cafés and camps still operate on the beachfront. ◈ *Map C2*

9 The Colored Canyon and Ain Khudra

Bedouin guides take tourists on amazing jeep tours and multi-day camel safaris through Sinai's oases and canyons. The Colored Canyon, named for the vivid swirls of pink, cream, and silver rock formations, is a popular day trip. Visits involve an hour's scramble in the sandstone gorge. Ain Khudra (Green Spring) is an isolated oasis of palms set in a spectacular white-and-red valley. Tours can be arranged from Dahab and Nuweiba. ◈ *Map C2*

Pharaoh's Island

10 Taba and Surrounds

The Taba border crossing between Egypt and Israel is open 24 hours. The town itself is unmemorable, but just south is the picturesque Pharaoh's Island. The Taba Heights resort, 11 miles (18 km) south, is a complex of luxury hotels. It is an all-inclusive experience, with watersports, golf, and diving safaris available. The coastline all the way to Tarabin is dotted with bedouin camps and beach huts. Most appealing, from north to south, are the beaches at Ras Shaitan, Bir Sweir, and Basata. ◈ *Map C2*

Trip to St. Catherine's Monastery

Morning

🕙 Instead of joining a tour, arrange a car and driver through your hotel, or ask a local bedouin. A minivan works out cheap shared between a few people. Aim to get to the Monastery by 10am. From **Dahab** it takes 2 hours, from **Sharm el-Sheikh** *(see p91)* at least 3, with enough time to admire desert and mountain views on the way. The Monastery is open till 11:45am, so there will be plenty of time to look around. Afterward, drive to the village of Al-Milga, a mile (2 km) away. There are stores selling water and snacks. Visit Fansina *(see p49)*, a bedouin shop selling quality handicrafts and textiles made by tribal women (open Sat–Thu until 3pm). Have lunch at one of several hotels in the village. Or, plan ahead and book lunch at the **Monastery Guesthouse** *(see p94)*.

Afternoon

Relax in the courtyard with a coffee for a while, before tackling **Mount Sinai** *(see p91)*. It takes around 2 to 3 hours to reach the summit and the sunset views are stunning. Start descending immediately after. You will need to keep up a steady pace to avoid getting stuck in the dark. Take a torch in any case. You can dine in Al-Milga, or pick up some snacks before heading back. People-watch while enjoying a cozy meal at **Blue House** *(see p95)* in Dahab, or treat yourself to Italian fare at **El Fanar** *(see p95)* in Sharm.

Left **Camel Bar** Right **Rooftop bar, Nesima Resort**

Bars and Nightlife

1 Terrazina Beach Club
This "dance beach" can veer into tackiness on a big party night, otherwise the music is good, and so are the special food and drink deals. ⊗ *Harbour Rd., Sharm el-Maiya • Map D2 • 0100 500 6621 • Open 8am–10pm daily*

2 Coffeeshops
Lit by fairy lights, scented by wafts of *sheesha toofah* (apple tobacco) smoke, and serving hot and cold drinks, coffeeshops are a big part of Egypt's culture. ⊗ *Old Market, Sharm el-Maiya and Naama Bay • Map D2*

3 Little Buddha
Dimly lit and funky, Little Buddha is known for Asian fusion food and sushi. ⊗ *Naama Bay, Sharm el-Sheikh • Map D2 • (069) 360 1030 • Open daily*

4 Pacha
Sharm's biggest nightclub for many years, this huge venue continues to attract top-notch DJs. ⊗ *Sanafir, Naama Bay, Sharm el-Sheikh • Map D2 • (069) 360 0197 • Open 11pm–4am daily*

5 Pataya Beach
This beach has a lounge-bar, an outdoor seafood restaurant, a pool, and sun loungers. Although it's a great place to relax most days, Wednesday and Friday nights are reserved for clubbing, with live DJs and performers. ⊗ *Nabq • Map D2 • (20) 100 979 7000 • Open 10am–2am*

6 Camel Bar
This diver-friendly haunt has an indoor bar hosting bands and sporting events, a terrace, and a chilled-out rooftop. Food is available. ⊗ *Naama Bay, Sharm el-Sheikh • Map D2 • (069) 360 0700 • Bar open 3:30pm daily, 1pm Sat & Sun; roof and terrace winter: 5pm, summer: 7pm*

7 Nesima Resort
The downstairs bar here is cozy and unpretentious, while the rooftop lounge-bar is great for an evening drink. ⊗ *Mashraba, Dahab • Map D2 • (069) 364 0320 • Open 7–10am & 11am–11pm*

8 Tree Bar
A relaxed, young, and friendly beachside bar-club, Tree Bar also plays decent dance music. ⊗ *Mashraba, Dahab • Map D2 • (20) 109 53 1105 • Open 2pm–3am daily*

9 El-Nakhil Inn
This is a very pleasant beach-bar for a sundowner. Views of the lights twinkling across the Red Sea and the globe-shaped candle-holders make it atmospheric. ⊗ *North end of Tarabin, Nuweiba • Map C2 • (069) 350 0879 • Open 8–11pm daily*

10 Monastery Guesthouse
The courtyard café at this guesthouse serves rather pricey beer, but it's certainly a lovely setting to enjoy a drink. ⊗ *St. Catherine's Monastery • Map D1 • (069) 347 0353 • Open 7am–late Mon–Sat, midnight–3am Fri & Sat*

Price Categories

For a three-course meal for one with half a bottle of wine (or equivalent meal), taxes, and extra charges.

$	under $15
$$	$15–25
$$$	$25–40
$$$$	$40–55
$$$$$	over $55

Above **Reef Grill**

🔟 Restaurants

1 El Masrien
Located on the edge of the Old Market, El Masrien attracts foreign and Egyptian tourists alike. It is famed for its grills and huge range of salads. ◉ *Old Market, Sharm al-Maiya • Map D2 • (069) 366 2904 • Open noon–4am • $$$*

2 Abou El-Sid
With a menu of classic Egyptian dishes, Abou El-Sid is perfect for trying traditional food. Alcohol and *shocsha* are served. ◉ *Naama Bay, Sharm el-Sheikh • Map D2 • (069) 360 3910 • Open noon–2am • $$$$*

3 Sala Thai
Overlooking the Red Sea, this is a sophisticated, romantic restaurant. Dishes are authentic, decor tasteful, and the staff attentive. ◉ *Hyatt Regency Sharm el-Sheikh Resort, Gardens Bay, Sharm el-Sheikh • Map D2 • (069) 360 1234 • Open 6–11pm • $$$$*

4 Rangoli
Authentic Indian cuisine, especially *tandoor* dishes, are on offer here. ◉ *Sofitel Sharm, 5.5 miles (9 km) N of Naama Bay, Sharm El Sheikh • Map D2 • (069) 360 0081 • Open 7–11:30pm • $$$$*

5 Reef Grill
Fish, seafood, and imported steaks dominate the menu at Reef Grill which has a picturesque setting near the beach. ◉ *Four Seasons Hotel, Sharm el-Sheikh • Map D2 • (069) 360 3555 • Open 12:30–4.30pm & 7–10pm • $$$$$ • www.fourseasons.com*

6 El Fanar
Serving delectable Italian food, this restaurant is stunningly located by a lighthouse. It also has beach space. ◉ *Ras Umm Sidd, Sharm el-Sheikh • Map D2 • (069) 366 2218 • Open noon–11pm • $$$$*

7 Blue House
This simple Thai eatery looks onto Dahab's promenade. The chef is Thai, and so the dishes taste truly genuine. ◉ *Seven Heaven Hotel, Masbat, Dahab • Map D2 • 016 717 7846 • $$*

8 Chillax Restaurant
It is worth visiting this place for the reliable Western menu. Sample the excellent burgers, sandwiches, and vegetarian snacks. ◉ *Dahab • Map D2 • (018) 241 6394 • $$*

9 Eel Garden Stars
This Dahab favorite is marginally pricier than the restaurants on the promenade, but the fresh, diverse menu and tranquil setting are far superior. ◉ *Assalah, north end of the beach, Dahab • Map D2 • (010) 375 2904 • Open 9am–late • $$$*

10 Castle Zaman
Housed in a beautifully crafted stone building, with a magical pool and sublime Red Sea views, Castle Zaman is famous for its slow-cooked meat and gourmet seafood meals. ◉ *1 mile (2 km) N of Basata • Map C1 • (018) 214 0591 • Open noon–10:30 pm • $$$$$*

Left **Elephant capital, Archaeological Museum** Center **The Monastery** Right **Entrance to the Siq**

Petra

THIS SPECTACULAR NABATAEAN CITY *was hewn out of red-rock mountains and sandstone gorges. One of the most atmospheric ancient sites in the world, the carved tombs and temples have sparked travelers' imaginations since their rediscovery in 1812. Built between the 3rd century BC and the 1st century AD, Petra became the capital of a vast trading empire. The Romans annexed the metropolis in AD 106, later the Byzantines later built churches here, and even the Crusaders passed through. Known as the "rose-red city,"*

the hills and valleys are patterned with swirls of colored stone that reflect attractively onto the monumental facades. Hiking here is a pleasure, with peripheral peaks, altars, and tombs offering greater challenges. Given the size of the site, visitors can easily spend several days here.

Mosaic, Petra Church

Sights

1 The Siq
2 The Treasury
3 The Theater
4 Qasr el-Bint
5 Petra Church
6 The Royal Tombs
7 The Monastery
8 Museums
9 High Place of Sacrifice
10 Little Petra

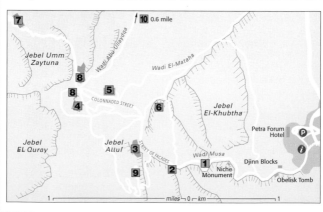

The Siq

The winding fissure of the Siq makes the last leg of the journey to Petra truly romantic. In places, the ravine is so narrow, that it feels cave-like. Placing the Treasury at the exit was a calculated move by the Nabataeans, for maximum visual impact. If you stay late at the site, walking back through the Siq in the sunset light is a real highlight. The thrice-weekly nighttime tours – when the Siq is lit by candles and silence is enforced – are beautiful, though the musical performance is brief. ✆ *Map B3*

The Treasury

One of the Middle East's most incredible sights, this temple was built in the 1st century BC. Its sudden materialization at the end of the Siq is unforgettable. The rose-pink facade, deeply recessed into the rock, is sharply chiseled into columns, two half-pediments, and horned capitals. The interior is simple by comparison. An outer court leads to the inner chamber with an ablution basin at the rear.

The glorious facade of the Treasury

Bedouins believed that the urn on top of the Treasury contained the hidden wealth of the pharaohs, so they shot at it in an attempt to dislodge it – hence the bulllet marks. ✆ *Map B3*

The Theater

The Theater

Scooped out of the mountainside, this Roman-style theater has seating for 7,000 people on 45 rows. Above, you can see the inside of several tombs. Their facades were cut away when the theater was built. Arched tunnels on either side allowed access to the stage, which was obscured from the Outer Siq by a wall. The theater probably dates to the 1st century AD, and was built by the Nabataeans. ✆ *Map B3*

Qasr el-Bint

The fanciful bedouin name "Qasr el-Bint el-Faroun" means the "Palace of the Pharaoh's Daughter." However, it is more likely that this grand edifice was the city's most sacred temple, built in the 1st century BC. The impressive Temenos Gate signals one's arrival at Qasr el-Bint's sacred precinct – it is still possible to make out remnants of the decorative plasterwork and marble veneers on the walls. The massive stone slab at the base of the steps was probably an altar to the sun god Dushara. The Crusaders used Qasr el-Bint as a stable. ✆ *Map B3*

Petra Church

One of several churches, the main Byzantine basilica dates from the 5th and 6th centuries AD. The well-preserved mosaic floors of the aisles, depicting deer, birds, and mythological creatures, are a highlight here. Human figures represent the seasons and elements of nature. In the nave, parts of the geometrical stone and marble floor have also survived. In 1993, a cache of 152 burnt scrolls was discovered at the church. These have given insights into the daily life of Byzantine Petra. ◈ *Map B3*

The Royal Tombs

The impressive scale of these tombs indicates they were built for Petra's most wealthy citizens. The largest is the Palace Tomb. Originally five storys high,
its top levels were raised up using huge blocks of stone. The Corinthian Tomb is badly eroded and unsymmetrical, but its design echoes that of the Treasury. A staircase leads up to the lofty Urn Tomb. Its interior was consecrated as a church in AD 447. The beauty of these tombs is enhanced by the vibrant stripes of color rippling over their walls and ceilings. They are especially magnificent when viewed from a distance in the afternoon sun. ◈ *Map B3*

The Monastery

This temple is one of Petra's most mesmerizing sights, second only to the Treasury in impact. The path up here is memorable too, ascending through a gorge and involving over 800 rock-cut steps. Of a similar Classical design to the Treasury, it's simpler but on a larger scale. Dedicated to the deified king Obodas I, who died in 86 BC, the facade hides one large chamber where an altar stood. The top is crowned by a colossal urn resting on ornate horned capitals. Carved into the mountains, which create a natural amphitheater around, the plateau has amazing views. ◈ *Map B3*

Museums

The Archaeological Museum is located inside a cave-tomb and displays relics excavated from the Petra region. Stone statuary includes the elephant capitals used to decorate buildings. The newer Nabataean Museum puts the history of Petra into context, and details specific excavation

The Royal Tombs

Bring a hat, sunscreen, and sunglasses with you.

sites. Among the artifacts displayed are jewelry, Edomite pottery, water pipes, figurines, and ancient coinage of the region. Note the marble basin with lioness handles that was found inside Petra Church. ◈ Map B3

High Place of Sacrifice

⑨ High Place of Sacrifice

This is the best preserved of Petra's sacrificial places. Animals and birds were sacrificed here. On the summit, two 20-ft (6-m) free-standing stone obelisks have been hewn out of the rock. Nearby is the High Place itself, demarcated by a large courtyard with a squat offering table. Steps lead to the main altar, with a rectangular indentation in the top. The adjacent round altar has a channel leading to a basin, possibly used for draining away the sacrificial blood. ◈ Map B3

⑩ Little Petra

Siq el-Berid (Cold Canyon) is commonly known as "Little Petra" as it looks like a mini replica of the main city. A small gorge containing an unadorned temple leads to the town, which was possibly where Petra's wealthiest merchants lived. Innumerable facades, temples, stairways, and cisterns greet visitors. A particular attraction is the Painted House. The plaster inside is adorned with grapevines, flowers, and images of Greek gods Eros and Pan.
◈ 5 miles (8 km) N of Wadi Musa

Walk to the High Place of Sacrifice

Morning

🕐 This walk takes 2–3 hours. Many paths used to lead to the **High Place of Sacrifice**, as it was Petra's most important cultic center. Now only two are accessible. The more impressive route begins shortly before **The Theater** *(see p97)*, marked at the start by **Djinn Blocks** *(see p28)*. The ascent is gradual but taxing. The summit, at 3,000 ft (914 m), is marked by a large terrace and two obelisks. Further north, a second plateau contains a rock-cut cistern and the two sacrificial altars of the High Place of Sacrifice. The views are great, stretching all the way to Aaron's Tomb, a white shrine at the top of Petra's highest peak. Follow the other path back down, which finishes in Wadi Farasa near **Qasr el-Bint** *(see p97)*. Steps go past the Lion Monument representing the goddess al-Uzza – water once poured from the lion's mouth. A series of steps then leads past colored rocks to the sheltered Garden Tomb, topped by a cistern. Further along, the Tomb of the Roman Soldier is named after the figure of a Roman official carved into a niche. A Triclinium, located on the opposite side of the tomb, has an ornately carved interior. Down the path is the Broken Pediment Tomb, and then the Renaissance Tomb. Three urns adorn the arched entrance. The track widens here, leading to the city of 📍 **Petra**. Stop for a bite at the Basin Restaurant at the far end of the City.

Aim to be first through the gates in the morning, to walk down the Siq without any tour groups.

STREETSMART

ISRAEL, SINAI & PETRA'S TOP 10

Left **Road sign in three languages** Center **Tourist Office, Jerusalem** Right **Three-pin plug**

Planning Your Trip

When to Go
Travel is possible all year, although July and August are extremely hot. Israel experiences some winter rain, while Sinai and Petra have almost none. Winter nights are cold in mountainous and desert areas. In Israel, Jewish and Christian holidays push flight and hotel prices up considerably.

What to Take
Warm clothing is essential during winter and for desert nights, and in summer sunglasses, a hat, sunscreen, and insect repellent are imperative. Bring a shawl to cover the head and arms in religious places. It is advisable to bring any prescription medicines from home. Carry your driver's license if you intend to rent a car.

Passports and Visas for Israel
All visitors need a passport that is valid for at least six months. Citizens of Western countries are given a free 3-month visa on arrival, while those from Arab, Asian, and African countries must obtain a visa from an Israeli consulate in their home country. Visas can be extended at offices of the Ministry of the Interior. ✆ www.mfa.gov.il

Passports and Visas for Sinai
When entering Sinai from Israel, a free 14-day "Sinai Permit" (covering the east coast and St. Catherine's Monastery) is issued at the Taba border. From Aqaba, Jordan, this permit is available on board the boat, or you can buy a "full visa" ($15) on disembarking at Nuweiba Port. Full visas can also be arranged at an Egyptian consulate in your home country, or (in a day) in Eilat.
✆ Egyptian Consulate in Eilat: 68 Efroni St. • Open 9:30am–noon Sun–Thu

Passports and Visas for Jordan
Tourists must have a passport valid for at least six months. One-month visas ($30) are issued at Queen Alia Airport, and the Wadi Arava and Sheikh Hussein border crossings. If entering Jordan at Allenby Bridge crossing, you must have your visa in advance. Visas can be issued by the Jordanian consulate in your home country, or in Tel Aviv.

Insurance
Health insurance with good cover is essential, since medical care is expensive in Israel, and a policy should cover the cost of a flight home. In Jordan and Sinai, government hospitals should be avoided, and the best doctors and private hospitals cost a lot of money. Travel insurance covering personal belongings, delay and cancellations is advised.

Customs
Duty-free allowance in Israel is 250 cigarettes and a liter of spirits or 2 liters of wine. In Egypt and Jordan it is 200 cigarettes and a liter of alcohol.

Time and Electricity
In all three countries, time is seven hours ahead of Eastern Standard Time (EST) and two hours ahead of Greenwich Mean Time (GMT). Daylight Saving Time is roughly from March to September. Electricity is 220V. Plugs in Israel are round-pronged and three-pinned; in Jordan and Sinai they are round-pronged and two-pinned.

Languages
English is widely spoken in both Israeli and Palestinian areas. Road signs are in Hebrew, Arabic, and English. In Sinai and Petra, it is easy to find English speakers. Attempts to speak Arabic or Hebrew are always appreciated.

Sources of Information
There are many excellent tourist offices in Israel, but few in Sinai. Various websites can be consulted for comprehensive travel information.
✆ www.gojerusalem.com
• www.telavivguide.net
• www.visit-tlv.com
• www.visitpalestine.ps
• www.petrapark.com

Left **A passport with entry stamps** Center **Ben Gurion Airport** Right **A** *sherut*

⑩ Getting There

1 From the Americas

The Israeli national airline El Al has flights from New York, Los Angeles, and Toronto, taking between 12 and 16 hours. Ben Gurion Airport is also served by American Airlines, Continental Airlines, and Delta. Fares include departure tax and are at a premium during holiday periods.

2 From Europe

El Al has direct flights from European cities taking between 3 and 6 hours. Ben Gurion is also served by Air France, Alitalia, British Airways, KLM, Lufthansa, and Swissair, as well as low-cost airlines such as Jet2 and easyJet from the UK. The Israeli airline Arkia is worth checking for cheap flights, and Israir serves a few European cities.

3 Packages and Charter Flights

Eilat's Ovda airport caters largely to charter traffic, and it is on these flights that the cheapest fares from Europe are found. The drawbacks are date restrictions, and having to make your own way to Jerusalem and back.
🕾 www.iaa.gov.il

4 Ben Gurion Airport

The airport is near Lod, some 14 miles (22 km) southeast of Tel Aviv and about 28 miles (45 km) from Jerusalem. Most international flights arrive at and depart from Terminal 3, which has duty-free, currency exchange, cell-phone rental, car hire, free Wi-Fi, and tourist information. The older Terminal 1 is used for domestic flights and for check-in of low-cost international airlines.
🕾 www.iaa.gov.il

5 Security Checks at Ben Gurion

Ben Gurion has the tightest airport security in the world. Check in three hours before departure, and be prepared for serious questioning and for every item of baggage to be searched.

6 To/From Jerusalem and Ben Gurion

Private taxis take about 45 minutes to Jerusalem, or you can take a *sherut* (shared taxi). *Sheruts* run all night and during Shabbat, and will take you anywhere in the city. To get to the airport from Jerusalem, book either a taxi or the Nesher *sherut* the day before departure. Hotels can arrange this, or call Nesher or the airport's licensed taxis.
🕾 Nesher: (02) 625 7227; www.neshertours.co.il
• Airport Licensed Taxis: (03) 975 9555

7 To/From Tel Aviv and Ben Gurion

There are no buses or *sheruts* between Tel Aviv and the airport. However, a 24-hour train service connects to all four stations in the city. From the railway stations, a private taxi, *sherut*, or bus can take you to a hotel.

8 Borders Between Israel and Jordan

There are three land borders between the two countries. Allenby Bridge (also known as King Hussein Bridge) is easily accessible from East Jerusalem, but Jordanian visas must be arranged in advance. The Jordan River Border Terminal (Sheikh Hussein Crossing) is close to Beth Shean in the north. Yitzhak Rabin Terminal (Wadi Arava) is the most southerly.

9 Crossing to Petra

The most convenient border crossing for Petra is Wadi Arava (Yitzhak Rabin Terminal), 2 miles (4 km) from Eilat and 6 miles (10 km) from Aqaba. Here, the Jordanians waive the entry tax but you have to pay the Israeli exit taxes.

10 Crossing to Sinai

The Taba border between Israel and Sinai is open 24 hours a day all year, except Yom Kippur and Eid al-Adha. Aqaba in Jordan and Nuweiba in Sinai are linked by ferry (3 hours) and catamaran (about 1 hour). The latter is only a little more expensive.

Left **An Egged Bus** Right **The Jerusalem Light Rail**

Getting Around

1 Long-Distance Buses

In Israel, Egged operates most long-distance buses. You buy a ticket from the driver on boarding. The only journey bookable in advance is to Eilat. Buses are comfortable and air-conditioned, but they do not run on Shabbat or on Jewish holidays.
 www.egged.co.il

2 Buses Around Jerusalem

Buses ply all the major sights, although from the Old City you often have to take the Light Rail to pick up a connecting bus. Journeys cost about $1.50, tickets are valid for both bus and tram for a 90-minute period. Arab buses leave from three stations outside Damascus Gate for the West Bank; just pay the driver on boarding.

3 Jerusalem Light Rail

The Light Rail has frequent trams (locals call them trains) between West and East Jerusalem that pass near the Old City and go the length of Jaffa Road. Armed security personnel are on board. The most useful stops for the Old City are City Hall and Damascus Gate. You can buy a ticket from automated machines on the platform, or get a Rav Kav card for discounted journeys.
 www.jet.org.il

4 Sheruts

A shared taxi is known to an Israeli as a *sherut* and to an Arab as a "service" (pronounced servees). There are no set stops, just tell the driver when you want to get off. Fares are similar to buses. *Sheruts* are particularly useful on Shabbat, when they run between major cities and within Tel Aviv's center.

5 Trains

Israel's railway system has six lines, with Tel Aviv acting as a hub. The coastal line north is the best way to travel to Haifa and Akko. Trains are crowded on Sunday morning and Thursday night, and they don't run during Shabbat. The Jerusalem–Tel Aviv train passes through some lovely scenery.
 www.rail.co.il

6 Taxis

Taxis are white with a yellow sign on top, which is lit up when they are available. Israeli drivers may sometimes refuse to drive to East Jerusalem, but Arab drivers are willing to go anywhere in West Jerusalem. Insist that meters in taxis are used. Fares are higher from 9pm–5:30am, during Shabbat, and on holidays.

7 Car Hire

Car hire offices are numerous throughout the country. Local companies, such as Eldan, usually offer the best rates. Be aware that rental charges are quoted exclusive of insurance and collision waivers. For two or more people it is a really economical way to see Israel. www.eldan.co.il

8 Coach Tours

This is an efficient way to see Israel. Tours are easily arranged through United Tours and Egged. Around Jerusalem, the No. 99 bus line for tourists stops at 24 key sights. www.unitedtours. co.il • www.eggedtours. com • www.abraham-hostel-jerusalem.com

9 Around Sinai

Car hire is not popular in Sinai as there are few roads, and drivers can be rather reckless. It is also expensive compared to other forms of transport, such as the bus or *sherut*, and is no cheaper than hiring a car with a driver for the day. Off-road driving should only be done with a local bedouin driver. East Delta bus stations: Sharm el-Sheikh (069) 366 0660; Dahab City (069) 364 1808

10 Around Petra

Petra is best explored on foot. Horse carriages for differently abled visitors can be hired at the visitors' center (see p28). Horses are also available for able-bodied visitors. Donkeys can be hired for the climb to the Monastery.

Left **Sign for wheelchair users** Right **Children in the Bloomfield Science Museum**

ᵀᴼᴾ10 Traveling Tips

1 Traveling With Children

Children are welcome at hotels and restaurants throughout this region. Familiar food is easy to find in Israel and at Sinai's resorts. Many museums in Israel have a children's section, and most sights offer discounted rates. Beaches, tunnels, camels, and ruined cities are appealing to young minds, but the summer heat may be unsuitable for some.

2 Budget Travelers

Cheap food can always be found, and transport is affordable throughout the region since there are buses to almost everywhere. In Israel, it's usually the price of accommodation that increases costs, although it is possible to sleep cheap (see p110).

3 Gay and Lesbian Travelers

Tel Aviv is among the world's top destinations for gay travelers. There is a Pride parade each June, and constant events and club nights. Conservative attitudes in Jerusalem mean it is inadvisable to flaunt same-sex relationships. In Palestinian areas, Jordan, and Sinai, homosexuality is not accepted.

4 Differently Abled Travelers

Many Israeli hotels and museums are equipped for disabled use, and national parks often have wheelchair routes. The Jerusalem Light Rail and the train network are wheelchair-friendly. Yad Sarah lends wheelchairs and other aids, and offers airport pickups. Some parts of Petra are accessible to the differently abled, and a few Sinai dive centers cater for disabled divers. Ⓢ *Yad Sarah: 124 Herzl Blvd., Jerusalem; (02) 644 4633*

5 Senior Citizens

Many elderly pilgrims find the cobbled stepped streets of Jerusalem's Old City challenging. However, pilgrim hospices lie within the Old City walls, meaning there is never too far to walk. Discounts are available.

6 Women Travelers

Lone females are occasionally subjected to verbal pestering and unwanted attention from local men. The problem is most acute in Jerusalem's Old City and on Sinai's beaches. Don't walk alone in secluded areas after dark, and ignore any inappropriate suggestions.

7 Kibbutz Volunteering

Working on a kibbutz is an option for people aged 19–35 years. There is a (reasonable) fee for the program, to cover visa services and medical insurance, and you receive food, lodging, and pocket money. It is advised to arrange a program before arrival. Ⓢ *www.kibbutzprogram center.org*

8 Volunteering in the Palestinian Territories

Volunteering opportunities abound in Palestinian towns and villages. Project Hope welcomes people aged over 21 years with some teaching experience to run various courses in Nablus. Volunteers are welcome at Cinema Jenin – a fascinating project. Ⓢ *www.projecthope.ps* • *www.cinemajenin.org*

9 Drugs and Alcohol

Drugs are illegal in this region, and penalties are harsh. In Sinai, marijuana is not uncommon but tolerant attitudes are a thing of the past. Alcohol is available in Israel, but it's not consumed in large quantities by locals. At Sinai's resorts, alcohol is commonplace but drunkenness is not. In Petra, expect alcohol only in larger hotels.

10 Political and Religious Issues

Both Israelis and Palestinians are used to political discourse. Aside from diverse opinions on how to find a solution to the conflict, there are huge gulfs between the different streams of Judaism. Use common sense in this region when expressing your views.

Left **An ATM in Tel Aviv** Center **Shekel coins** Right **Newspapers for sale in Haifa**

TOP 10 Banking and Communications

1 Banks and ATMs
Israeli banks open Monday to Thursday from 9am to 1pm. They shut Fridays and Saturdays, as do banks in Jordan. ATMs linked into international banking networks are widespread in Israel, and some dispense US dollars and euros. All major tourist spots in Sinai have reliable ATMs.

2 Currencies
Israel's currency is the new Israeli shekel (NIS). It is also used in the Palestinian Territories. Jordan has dinars (JD), and Sinai has the Egyptian pound (LE). Exchange rates between the three tend to be bad, so use up all your NIS before leaving Israel, and change dollars for JD or LE in Jordan or Sinai.

3 Exchange
Cash can be changed at banks, exchange offices, and hotels. Note that rates vary and, in Israel, it is best to use a licensed exchange or post office, which don't charge a commission. You can buy JD at money-changers around Damascus Gate in Jerusalem, but LE can only be bought at the border or within Sinai.

4 Credit/Debit Cards
Major credit cards, such as VISA and MasterCard, are widely accepted throughout Israel in shops, restau-rants, and hotels. In Petra and Sinai, most large hotels, restaurants, and travel agents accept credit cards, but carry plenty of cash while visiting smaller places. Debit cards are rarely used for purchases but can be used in ATMs.

5 Phone Codes
The country code for Israel is 972. In the Palestinian territories the code is also 972, or 970 from some Arab countries. Jordan's country code is 962, and the area code for Petra and Aqaba is 03. Egypt's country code is 20, and Sinai has the area code 069. ✆ *Area codes: Jerusalem (02); Tel Aviv (03); Galilee and the north (04); Dead Sea and the south (08)*

6 Phones (Israel)
Rent cell phones with local sim cards at the airport. Rental rates start at $1 per day, plus the cost of calls. You can also buy a local sim and pay-as-you-go. Israeli net-works' coverage extends to the Palestinian territories, and vice-versa. To dial abroad use the international access codes 012, 013, or 014. ✆ *www.israelphones.com*

7 Phones (Jordan and Sinai)
Pay-as-you-go sim cards are the cheapest option. In Sinai, numerous shops and kiosks sell them. You can buy credit electronically or with vouchers. Most hotels provide an international line, but it is expensive.

8 Post
Israeli post offices are always terribly busy. A standard airmail letter to the US or Europe costs about $1. In Jordan, posting letters at a 5-star hotel or main post office is better than using a post box. Postcards from Sinai are most easily sent from hotels, and shops sell stamps.

9 Internet
Internet cafés are rare in Israel, but free Wi-Fi is ubiquitous in bars and restaurants. Ben Yehuda Street in Jerusalem and Rothschild Boulevard in Tel Aviv have free Wi-Fi, and hotels and hostels either offer access to Wi-Fi or computers. In Palestinian areas, Internet cafés are prevalent, as they are in Wadi Musa (Petra). In Sinai, free Wi-Fi is common in restaurants and hotels.

10 Newspapers and Magazines
The *Jerusalem Post* and *Haaretz* are published in English. *Time Out Israel* is an excellent magazine available at tourist offices and hotels. *This Week in Palestine* is available in East Jerusalem, and lists events. The *Jordan Times* is worth picking up, and in Sinai foreign newspapers are widely available.

Left **Ambulance, Nazareth** Center **Israeli policemen** Right **Pharmacy sign**

🔟 Security and Health

1 Terrorism and Security Issues

Acts of terrorism are rare now in Israel and never target tourists. However, always get local opinion before visiting sensitive places like the Haram esh-Sharif and Hebron. There are security checks when entering bus stations and malls, and some hotels in Sharm el-Sheikh screen visitors on entry. Keep abreast of the security situation before and during travel.

2 Police and Security Forces

Special tourist police are posted at major sites throughout the region; report any problems to them. Israeli police wear navy blue, and border police wear grey. Armed personnel are ever-present, especially in the Old City. The Palestinians have their own forces within autonomous areas.
● *Police Jerusalem: 100* • *Petra 199* • *Sinai: 122*

3 Documentation

Carry your passport at all times. It is required when crossing into the West Bank, and to gain admittance to some museums. In Sinai you need to produce it when traveling up and down the coast or going to St. Catherine's Monastery.

4 Theft

Visitors to the region rarely encounter crime and in general, Israelis and Arabs are extremely honest. To minimize risks, do not leave valuables in full view in hotel rooms and never leave them unattended inside a car. In case of theft, remember to get a police report to make an insurance claim.

5 Hitchhiking

Known as *tremping* in Israel, hitchhiking used to be a common way to get around. However, it is now considered unsafe for lone travelers. If you flag down a lift in Sinai and Jordan, you will be expected to negotiate a suitable payment.

6 Water

It is safe to drink tap water in Israel, although locals filter it as it is chlorinated. In Sinai and Petra, buy bottled water, which is available in stores and hotels. Some restaurants provide filtered water but if in doubt, stick to the bottled variety. Avoid ice.

7 Heat and Sun Precautions

The hot climate necessitates drinking large volumes of water, particularly in desert areas. Harsh light can damage eyes, so pack quality sunglasses. You will find little shade while walking around Petra, or on Sinai desert excursions, so wear a hat and plenty of sunscreen.

8 Hospitals and Pharmacies

Hospitals in Israel provide excellent care, but treatment is expensive. In Sinai, Sharm el-Sheikh has the modern South Sinai Hospital, but in Petra and Aqaba there are only state hospitals. In Jordan, if you need a doctor, ask in a pharmacy or hotel for a recommendation. Most large hotels in Sinai have a resident doctor. Good pharmacies are easy to find in all three countries.
● *Ambulance Israel (101); Petra (199); Sinai (123)* • *South Sinai Hospital: Salem Rd., El Nour; (069) 366 6020/30/40; www.southsinaihospital.com*

9 Hyperbaric Chambers

Divers should note that there are two facilities in Sharm el-Sheikh equipped with recompression chambers – the Hyperbaric Medical Center and the International Hospital. In Eilat, a decompression chamber and trained medical team are on call 24/7. ● *Hyperbaric Medical Center: Sharm el-Maya; (+20) 12 212 4929*

10 Embassies

Most countries have embassies in Tel Aviv, and a few have consular offices in Jerusalem. There is an Egyptian consulate in Eilat, and at Aqaba in Jordan. No embassies have representation in Sinai.
● *www.embassyworld.com*

Left **Crowds in the Old City, Jerusalem** Right **Visitors with covered heads, Western Wall**

Things to Avoid

1 Inappropriate Dress

All religious places require visitors to dress suitably; shorts and bare shoulders are not acceptable. Head-coverings are usually provided at religious sites. Wearing inappropriate clothing is considered disrespectful, and will result in entrance being denied. Also dress modestly when visiting Islamic and Orthodox Jewish neighborhoods.

2 Israeli Passport Stamp

An Israeli stamp in your passport will bar you from entering most Arab countries, notably Syria, Lebanon, and Sudan. To avoid this, ask the officer at passport control not to stamp your passport. Make the same request on exiting. At land borders, you may have to fill in a form, which is then stamped with the visa.

3 Dehydration and Sunstroke

Dehydration is a real threat, particularly in desert areas. Always carry bottles of mineral water, wear a hat and sunscreen, and avoid exerting yourself in the midday heat.

4 Photography in Sensitive Areas

Photography is not permitted at military installations in this region. In Israel, yellow signs are clearly displayed to alert

visitors to such prohibitions. When photographing people, particularly women in Arab areas, always ask for permission first.

5 Crowds at Tourist Sights

Fridays and Saturdays are the busiest days at secular tourist sights and national parks in Israel. Mahane Yehuda in Jerusalem is packed on Thursday afternoons and Friday mornings. St. Catherine's Monastery is always busy due to it's limited opening hours, although the masses thin out later in the morning. At Petra, start at dawn to avoid tourist traffic.

6 Public Displays of Affection

Jerusalem is much more conservative than the rest of secular Israel, and in Orthodox areas segregation of the sexes is customary. Intimate physical contact in public is taboo in Arab regions, with the exception of some Sinai beaches. Kissing or even holding hands can cause offense.

7 Traveling on Shabbat

There is a total shutdown of bus and train services during Shabbat. Make sure to plan any journeys in advance, and enquire at your hotel about *sheruts (see p104)*. During Shabbat hours, taxis charge higher fares.

8 Touts

Potential problems in Jerusalem's Old City are would-be guides and aggressive vendors. Similarly, in Sinai and Petra, over-friendly locals usually have little of any worth to offer. Politely refuse services that are of no interest to you. Be forewarned that goods will be low quality, and that guides are better arranged through your hotel or an agency.

9 Being Ripped Off

Shopkeepers in the Old City quote prices that are way above the actual value of the goods, so haggle hard. Souvenirs are cheaper in Bethlehem or Hebron, and there are shops that pay fair prices to the artisans whose wares they sell. Be equally wary of inflated prices in Sinai's markets. When dining out, always check your bill and the change.

10 Overstaying Your Visa

Israeli visas can be extended at the Ministry of the Interior offices in major cities. This is advisable, rather than risking large fines at the airport. If traveling out via a land border, you can be refused exit with an expired visa. Free "Sinai permits" cannot be extended, but a "full Egypt visa" can. Overstaying by up to 15 days on a full Egypt visa only incurs a fine on exit.

Left **A happy hour sign** Center **Kosher restaurant** Right **Pavement café, Jerusalem**

TOP 10 Dining and Drinking Tips

1 Types of Restaurant

Top-end dining in Israel includes gourmet restaurants serving New Israeli Cuisine, where prior reservations are essential. Smaller restaurants specialize in traditional Jewish ethnic cuisines, such as Ashkenazi, Kurdish, or Moroccan. International restaurants are plentiful. Middle Eastern food dominates in Arab areas, except in Sinai, where restaurant menus represent global cuisine.

2 Kosher Restaurants

Jewish dietary laws of *kashruth* are observed in most restaurants, which means that pork and most seafood is forbidden, and that meat and dairy cannot be eaten together. Restaurants display certificates attesting to their Kosher credentials.

3 Dress Codes

The casual Israeli attitude extends to dining out. Even top restaurants wouldn't turn away guests wearing shorts. The resorts in Sinai are also used to casual dressing.

4 Vegetarians

There are several purely vegetarian/vegan restaurants in Israel, and hundreds more Kosher "dairy restaurants" that do not serve any meat. In Egypt and Jordan, vegetarianism is not a familiar concept, although many local dishes are, in fact, meat-free, such as *fuul* (fava beans) and falafel. Generous servings of *meze,* which include many vegetarian dishes, can fill anyone up.

5 Budget Dining

Israel has numerous cheap eateries and takeaways offering falafel, *shawarma,* hummus, or pizza slices. Many top restaurants have "business lunch" deals on weekdays. Look for discount vouchers on restaurants' websites and pick up *Jerusalem Menus* which has discount coupons inside. In Sinai, backpacker-oriented beach cafés serve inexpensive meals.

6 Alcohol

Alcohol is expensive in Israel, so look out for Happy Hours with two-for-one or half-price offers. In Tel Aviv, bars stay open until the last customer leaves. In Sinai, local Stella and Saqqara beers are inexpensive. However, in remote coastal camps, you might have to search for booze and pay premium prices for it.

7 Cafés and Coffee Shops

All Israeli cafés serve light meals. Tel Aviv is awash with pavement cafés, most of which are quirky and independent. In Jerusalem's Old City, there are several Arab coffee shops that serve Turkish-style coffee and where smoking *nargilla* (water pipes) is popular. Coffee shops in Sinai serve traditional drinks, and different flavors of *sheesha* (water pipes).

8 Smoking

In Israel, restaurants may have a separate smoking section, but more common are outdoor terraces where smoking is permitted. In Egypt and Jordan, smoking is allowed in almost all restaurants and bars, while in coffee shops it is encouraged. But during Ramadan, smoking is not permitted for Muslims, and tourists should similarly abstain.

9 Food Hygiene

Be sure to wash fruit and salad first before eating. In Sinai and Petra, it is unwise to eat salads in small local restaurants, as ingredients will have been rinsed under the tap. Be wary of buffets in lower-end hotels, where the food may have been left sitting for too long.

10 Taxes and Tipping

In Israel, it is customary to leave a 10–15 percent tip for good service. In Egypt, restaurants are subject to sales and service taxes which add nearly 25 percent to the bill. Menus should state whether prices include taxes. In addition to the service charge, a 10 percent tip is expected.

Left **A shop in Ben Yehuda Street, Jerusalem** Center **A Kibbutz-run hotel** Right **Austrian Hospice**

TOP 10 Accommodation & Shopping Tips

Reservations
Booking ahead is advised at all times and is absolutely essential during Christian and Jewish holidays. During Passover and Easter in particular, finding accommodations in Jerusalem can be a real problem, so plan your visit in advance. Almost all hotels and hostels have online booking.

Types of Hotels
Most Israeli hotels fall within the medium to high price range, with amenities to match and breakfast included. Kibbutz-run hotels offer a unique experience, and also peculiar to Israel are "zimmers," which tend to be cabin-style rural retreats offering B&B. In Sinai, five-star standards cost less and resorts are often fully-inclusive.
§ www.kibbutz.co.il
• www.zimmeril.com

Pilgrim Hospices
The various Christian communities run pilgrim hospices in Jerusalem and other holy towns. These are comfortable hostels also catering to tourists. Do not expect pools, gyms, or even a TV in the room, and be prepared for religious groups and possibly curfews. The advantage is their location: in historic buildings, near the main sights. It is essential to book hospices far in advance.

Budget Stays
Jerusalem and Tel Aviv have plenty of budget beds. The Israel Hostels organization (ILH) also provides accommodations that suit various budgets, but always have excellent dormitory and self-catering facilities. There are plenty of accommodations near Petra for backpackers, and Sinai beach huts cost less than $5 a night. § www.hostels-israel.com • www.iyha.org.il • www.hostelworld.com

Staying in the Palestinian Territories
Most tourists visit the West Bank sights from a base in Jerusalem, but for overnight stays there are plenty of good hotels and guesthouses. These are delighted to host independent travelers.
§ www.visitpalestine.ps
• www.toursinenglish.com

VAT Exclusions
Tourists to Israel are exempt from paying VAT (16 percent) on overnight accommodations, and on food, laundry, or use of other services in the hotel. In Eilat, VAT is exempted on all goods and services for everyone.

VAT Refunds
In Israel, tourists are entitled to a VAT refund on merchandise exceeding 400 NIS (about $100). You should receive a special VAT refund invoice with your purchases. Present this, sealed in a bag with the goods, at the VAT refund counter at the airport on departure.

Opening Hours
In Israel, most shops open from 9am to 7pm, although the Old City souks open around 10am until sunset. Christian-owned stalls are closed on Sundays, while those in the Muslim Quarter close on Fridays. Jewish shops are closed from Friday afternoon until sunset on Saturday for Shabbat. Shopkeepers of the various faiths close for religious holidays.

Haggling
Haggling is a Middle Eastern ritual. Never accept the first price given, as it will be way over the odds. Ask for prices at several stalls, decide what you are prepared to pay, and make an offer well below it. Bargain till you arrive at a mutually agreeable sum.

Where to Shop
Shop for souvenirs in the Arab souks, and explore Mahane Yehuda for everything from fresh produce to spices and homewares. Mamilla Avenue has Jerusalem's smartest shops, but Tel Aviv is better for fashion and design. Israel has many malls containing local chain stores. In Sinai, Dahab has many souvenir shops.

Left **Tourists in Petra** Right **Cyclist from Hooha cyclists' club**

TOP 10 Tours and Special Interests

1 Cycling
Bike touring is a great way to experience Israel, with challenging terrain and diverse scenery. In the West Bank, Bike Palestine offer tours off the beaten track. Tel Aviv has a scheme with 150 locations throughout the city where travelers can pick up and drop off bikes (for a fee). In city centers, stick to sidewalks and cycle paths for safety. ◈ www.ibike.co.il • www.geo fun.co.il • www.hooha.co.il • www.bikepalestine.com

2 Trekking
This region offers great opportunities for trekkers. In Israel, the SPNI are a good source of information. Within the West Bank, guided hikes are organized by Walk Palestine. Hiking through the mountain scenery of South Sinai can easily be arranged, while a visit to Petra naturally involves much trekking. ◈ SPNI: 13 Heleni HaMalkha St., Jerusalem; www.teva.org.il • www.walkpalestine.com • www.sheikhmousa.com

3 Palestinian Perspective Tours
Several companies offer tours in the West Bank. Good service and interesting itineraries are offered by Green Olive Tours, and Abraham Hostel in Jerusalem organizes a range of trips. ◈ www.toursinenglish.com • www.abraham-hostel-jerusalem.com

4 Taglit-Birthright Israel
Thousands of Jewish youngsters from around the world visit Israel on the Taglit-Birthright program. The free 10-day trip is educational and aims to strengthen their Jewish identity and connection with Israel. Apply through their website. ◈ www.birthrighisrael.com

5 Christian Pilgrimages
Numerous companies offer pilgrim tours, usually lasting between 5 and 10 days. Following in Jesus's footsteps through Jerusalem, Galilee, and the West Bank, tours often include visits to other important historical sites such as Caesarea, Masada, or even Tel Aviv. Accommodation is at the relevant denomination's hospice and the schedules are fairly grueling.

6 Eco-Touring
Israel is not a front-runner in environmental issues, but you can always find ways to have an eco-friendly holiday. An ecological experience is possible at Kibbutz Lotan in the Negev – a green community that offers activities and accommodations. ◈ www.kibbutzlotan.com

7 St. Catherine's Tours
A tour to St. Catherine's can be arranged from Eilat, or from Dahab or Sharm el-Sheikh. Note that tours from Eilat often don't include border taxes, which add at least $60 to the price. Tours arranged in Sinai usually include walking up the mountain at sunrise, followed by a morning visit to the monastery.

8 Petra Tours
Tours from Eilat are offered for 1–3 days; however, the price of a single-day ticket for Petra is so high that it makes economic sense to spend two days there. Again, border taxes can add a further $60 to the quoted price. ◈ www.fun-time.co.il

9 Diving
It is best to book a package from home. This will get you great deals on accommodations, as well as dive packages or PADI courses. Diving is cheaper and more varied in Sinai, although some dive shops in Eilat offer live-aboard trips along the Gulf of Aqaba. ◈ www.padi.com

10 Bird-Watching
Israel has year-round birding activity, with fall and spring being the peak seasons. Eilat and the Hula Valley are the prime locations, Mount Hermon, Beth Shean valley, and the Arava are also rewarding. ◈ www.israbirding.com • www.carmelbirdingtours.com

Left **Spa, Mamilla Hotel** Right **Cellar Bar, American Colony**

TOP 10 Characterful Hotels in Jerusalem

1 King David Hotel
This stately hotel with a splendid terrace, pool, and gardens overlooks the Old City. The plush rooms have antique furnishings and service is impeccable. Rooms with Old City views cost more. 🔎 *23 King David St. • Map M5 • (03) 520 2552, (02) 620 8888 • www. danhotels.com • $$$$$*

2 Mamilla Hotel
Chic, contemporary, and with high-tech amenities, the Mamilla enjoys an excellent location near Jaffa Gate. The pool is divine, and the drinking and dining options superb. Note that the sumptuous spa gets heavily booked and the studio rooms are small. 🔎 *11 King Solomon St. • Map M5 • (02) 548 2200, (02) 548 2222 • www. mamillahotel.com • $$$$$*

3 Hotel Alegra
Located 4 miles (7 km) west of Jerusalem in a quaint village, Alegra is a boutique hotel. The seven rooms are unique and luxurious. Spa treatments, a sauna, a sun roof, a magical garden, and their top-class restaurant enrich the experience. 🔎 *13 Ha'achayot St., Ein Karem • Map F4 • (02) 650 0506 • www.hotelalegra. co.il • $$$$$*

4 American Colony
This landmark hotel in East Jerusalem combines luxury, elegance, and class. The courtyard, garden, and Cellar Bar are a delight and rooms are tasteful. There's a pool (in season) and a fitness center. 🔎 *1 Louis Vincent St., Sheikh Jarrah, East Jerusalem • Map N1 • (02) 627 9777 • www. americancolony.com • $$$$$*

5 Harmony Hotel
A smooth white foyer sets the modish tone of this boutique hotel with 50 rooms, in the heart of the New City. The lounge has a pool table and outdoor seating. The breakfasts are great, as is the service, and amenities include free Wi-Fi and parking. 🔎 *6 Yoel Moshe Salomon St., Nakhalat Shiva • Map M3 • (02) 621 9999 • www. atlas.co.il/harmony-hotel-jerusalem • $$$$*

6 Montefiore Hotel
Modern and gracious, Montefiore is great value – with comfy beds and good bathrooms. Shatz Street has many restaurants and shops, and the Old City is nearby. 🔎 *7 Shatz St., West Jerusalem • Map L4 • (02) 622 1111 • www.montefiorehotel. com • $$$$*

7 Mount Zion Hotel
Poised over Mount Zion and the Hinnom Valley, this hotel is within easy distance of both the Old City and New City. The spa and fitness center are not state-of-the-art, and rooms are dated, but the pool and garden are a bonus 🔎 *17 Hebron Rd. • Map N6 • (02) 568 9555 • www. mountzion.co.il • $$$$*

8 Dan Boutique
This hotel is comfortable, jazzy, and informal. Standard rooms are a decent size, as are bathrooms, and have art and high-tech design features. The lively German Colony is close by. 🔎 *31 Hebron Rd. • Map N6 • (03) 520 2552 • www.danhotels.com • $$$$*

9 YMCA Three Arches
An iconic building known as Yimca, this is a classic place to stay in West Jerusalem. Its architecture is magnificent, but the rooms here need to be refurbished. The restaurant is reasonably priced. Come for the historic charm. 🔎 *26 King David St. • Map M5 • (02) 569 2692 • www. ymca3arch.co.il • $$$$*

10 Legacy
The ex-YMCA in East Jerusalem is a great mid-range option. Its institutional 1960s exterior hides a contemporary and bright interior, although some rooms are small. There's an indoor pool and the Damascus Gate is close by. 🔎 *29 Nablus St., East Jerusalem • Map N2 • (02) 627 0800 • www.jerusalem legacy.com • $$$$*

Above **Abraham Hostel**

Price Categories

For a standard double room per night (with breakfast if included), taxes, and extra charges.

$	under $50
$$	$50–110
$$$	$110–210
$$$$	$210–350
$$$$$	over $350

TOP 10 Pilgrim Hospices & Budget Stays

1 Notre Dame of Jerusalem Guesthouse

This magnificent edifice is a step away from New Gate, and views from the rooftop restaurant are great. Rooms are simple, beds comfy, and the breakfasts hearty. ◎ *3 HaTsankhanim • Map N4 • (02) 627 9111 • www.notre damecenter.org • $$$$*

2 St. George's Cathedral Pilgrim Guesthouse

Located near Damascus Gate, this guesthouse has a cloistered charm. Rooms are spacious and some have Jerusalem-stone walls. There's a courtyard garden, free Wi-Fi, and the Anglican cathedral exudes atmosphere. ◎ *20 Nablus Rd., East Jerusalem • Map N2 • (02) 628 3302 • www.j-diocese.org • $$$*

3 St. Andrew's Scottish Guesthouse

This small guesthouse adjoins the stark Scottish church. Rooms have either garden or Old City views, while the terrace and colonial lounge are nice spots to relax. ◎ *1 David Ramez St. • Map N6 • (02) 673 2401 • www. scotsguesthouse.com • $$$*

4 Austrian Hospice

Built in 1857 in the style of a Viennese Ring palace, this hostel welcomes independent travelers. The beds in the simple rooms are comfortable, and dorms are available. A prime location meets excellent value here, and the gardens, café-bar, and great views from the roof are added attractions. ◎ *37 Via Dolorosa, Old City • Map P4 • (02) 626 5800 • www.austrianhospice. com • $$$ Dorms $*

5 Christchurch Guesthouse

The location (just inside Jaffa Gate) couldn't be better, and the grounds are a haven. Rooms are simple but quaint. Unmarried couples are not allowed and there's an 11pm curfew. ◎ *Omar Ibn al-Khattab Sq., Jaffa Gate, Old City • Map P4 • (02) 627 7727 • www. cmj-israel.org • $$$*

6 Armenian Guest House

With clean and spacious rooms and dormitories, this hospice welcomes all creeds and religions. The courtyard restaurant serves Oriental food. Ask for a renovated room. ◎ *36 Via Dolorosa, Old City • Map P4 • (02) 626 0880 • $$$ Dorms $ • armenian guesthouse@hotmail.com*

7 Ecce Homo Convent Pilgrim House

Crucifixes adorn walls, terraces boast majestic views, and the staff are friendly at this dignified pilgrim house. Rooms are spotless, spartan, and very good value, so are the dormitories. The complex incorporates the Ecce Homo Arch and a basilica. ◎ *41 Via Dolorosa, Old City • Map P4 • (02) 627 7292 • www.eccehomo convent.org • $$ Dorms $*

8 Lutheran Guesthouse

Located in the Old City's heart, this 1860 guesthouse offers historic charm for a very reasonable price. Spotless rooms around a peaceful courtyard have A/C, and there's TV in the lounge. ◎ *7 St Marks St., Old City • Map P4 • (02) 626 6888 • www.guesthouse-jerusalem.com • $$*

9 Abraham Hostel

A large hostel with everything independent travelers need – sociable areas, a bar, breakfast, laundry facilities, tours, and free Wi-Fi. There are functional private rooms and dorms of varying sizes. ◎ *67 HaNevi'im St., Davidka Sq., West Jerusalem • Map L2 • (02) 650 2200 • www.abrahamhostel.com • $$ Dorms $*

10 Citadel Youth Hostel

Despite modest rooms and dorms, this warren-like hostel of Jerusalem stone has true character. The lack of breakfast is compensated for by free Wi-Fi. ◎ *20 St. Mark St., Old City • Map J2 • (02) 628 4494 • $$ Dorms $ • citadelhostel@yahoo.com*

Left **Montefiore Hotel** Right **Lounge, Brown TLV Urban Hotel**

TOP 10 Hotels and Hostels in Tel Aviv

1 Hotel Montefiore
Located in a 1920s building, this stylish hotel provides amazing service and exacting attention to detail. The chic resto-bar attracts celebrities, tourists, and locals alike. Great breakfasts. ✆ *36 Montefiore St. • Map V4 • (03) 564 6100 • www.hotel montefiore.co.il • $$$$$*

2 Dan Tel Aviv
One of the large chain hotels along Tel Aviv's shoreline, the Dan is an Israeli classic. It combines excellent service with smart dining and bars, attractive pools, terrific amenities, and a Mediterranean vibe. ✆ *99 HaYarkon St. • Map U2 • (03) 520 2552 • www. danhotels.com • $$$$$*

3 The Diaghilev Live Art Boutique Hotel
On a quiet leafy street, this contemporary hotel hosts art exhibitions. Accommodations are apartment-style, with kitchenettes and huge windows; rooms with balconies cost more. The airy foyer and rear deck are great spots to relax, and customer service is excellent. ✆ *56 Maze St. • Map W4• (03) 545 3131 • www.diaghilev.co.il • $$$$$*

4 Gordon Hotel and Lounge
This ultra-modern 12-room boutique hotel is right by the beach. The crisp white-and-black rooms are hip and high-tech, but rather on the small side. ✆ *2 Gordon St./136 HaYarkon St. • Map V1 • (03) 520 6100 • www. gordontlv.com • $$$$*

5 Center Chic
Housed in a striking Bauhaus building in the city centre, this hotel has undergone a makeover. Dog-tooth patterns meet bright hues, while art adorns white-brick walls in most rooms. A flower-filled roof terrace has loungers and citrus trees. Breakfast is served at the adjacent Cinema Hotel. ✆ *Kikar Dizengoff, 2 Zamenhoff St. • Map V2 • (03) 526 6100 • www.atlas.co.il • $$$$*

6 Shalom Hotel & Relax
Close to the sea, this hotel has a calming decor and a decked roof terrace. Some bathrooms here are a tight fit. The ambience is pure Mediterranean and, as in all Atlas hotels, there is a daily happy hour with complimentary drinks and snacks. ✆ *216 HaYarkon St. • Map E3 • (03) 542 5555, (03) 762 5400 • www.atlas.co.il • $$$$*

7 Brown TLV Urban Hotel
Dark brown walls and flooring create the mood, and the staff is lovely. Artwork enhances public and private spaces, and there is a spa, a court-yard, and a sundeck. Standard rooms are a bit small, but the location near Carmel Market is spot on. ✆ *25 Kalisher St. • Map V4 • (03) 717 0200 • www.browntlv.com • $$$$*

8 Port Hotel
Close to the *namal* (port), this intimate hotel is quite affordable. The decor is modern and stylish although some rooms are dark. The rooftop offers great sunset views and there's free Wi-Fi and bicycles. Cafés and bars are close by. ✆ *4 Yirmeyahu St., • Map E3 • (03) 544 5544 • www.porthoteltelaviv.com • $$$*

9 Beit Immanuel Guest House and Youth Hostel
This guesthouse is located in a historic building once owned by the Ustinovs. Large, plain private rooms and dorms, free Wi-Fi, and a garden café are on offer. No TV. ✆ *8 Auerbach St., American-German Colony • Map U5 • (03) 682 1459 • www. beitimmanuel.org • $$ Dorms $*

10 Hayarkon 48
The city's most popular hostel, located near the beach, is perfect for the independent traveler. Dorms and private rooms are clean, and there's a sociable lounge, a well-equipped kitchen, and free Wi-Fi. ✆ *48 HaYarkon St. • Map U3 • (03) 516 8989 • www.ha yarkon48.com • $$ Dorms $*

Price Categories		
For a standard double room per night (with breakfast if included), taxes, and extra charges.	**$** under $50	
	$$	$50–110
	$$$	$110–210
	$$$$	$210–350
	$$$$$	over $350

Above **Villa Carmel**

TOP10 Lodgings in Galilee and the North

Akkotel
Housed within the walls of the Old City in Akko, this 16-room hotel has a family feel, attentive staff, and a splendid third-floor terrace. Modcons add comfort to the quirky, pleasant rooms. ◈ *Salahuddin St., Old City, Akko • Map B4 • (04) 987 7100 • www.akkotel.com • $$$$*

Villa Carmel
This 1940s hotel is tucked away on the summit of Mount Carmel. The pleasant decor in the rooms is enhanced by luxuriant bedding. The sundeck, with a sauna and Jacuzzi, and fragrant gardens, are sublime. ◈ *1 Heinrich Heine St., Off 30 Moriah Boulevard), Haifa • Map C3 • (04) 837 5777/8 • www.villacarmel. co.il • $$$$$*

Colony Hotel
Set in the delightfully preserved German Colony, this hotel enjoys a great locale. Rooms are swish, with marble bathrooms, classy facilities, and a balcony if you're lucky. The Baha'i Gardens dominate the view from the roof. ◈ *28 Ben-Gurion Boulevard, Haifa • Map C3 • (04) 851 3344 • www.colonyhaifa.com • $$$$*

Scots Hotel
This deluxe hotel blends historic buildings with modern 5-star facilities. The "antique rooms" with basalt stone walls are the most attractive, and the seasonal pool and terraced gardens are divine. Cultural events, concerts, and brunches add to the special atmosphere. ◈ *1 Gedud Barak Rd., Tiberias • Map C5 • (04) 671 0701 • www. scotshotels.co.il • $$$$$*

YMCA Peniel-by-Galilee
The foyer here is an arabesque delight, while rooms are expansive but basic. The luxuriant gardens are lapped by the waters of the Kinneret. Service isn't very polished, but this is a quirky and restful place. ◈ *3 miles (5 km) north of Tiberias • Map C5 • (04) 672 0685 • www. ymca-galilee.co.il • $$$*

Pilgerhaus Tabgha
An unusual 19th-century building on the shores of the Sea of Galilee houses this hotel. Rooms are well-appointed and modern, while outdoor areas – including the bar – are great for relaxation. ◈ *Migdal-Tabgha, Galilee • Map B5 • (04) 670 0100 • www. heilig-land-verein.de • $$$$*

Artists' Colony Inn
With four huge rooms with arched stone walls, this hotel is located in the paved alleyways of the Artists' Quarter. Cute courtyards, superlative breakfasts, and attentive service, all make for a memorable stay. ◈ *9 Simtat Yud Zayin, Safed • Map B5 • (04) 604 1101 • www.artcol.co.il • $$$$*

Hotel Spa Mizpe Hayamim
Famed for its spa and organic farm, this hotel has rooms with classic furnishings, and lovely views over the Galilee. Fresh produce from the orchards, dairy, and the vegetable and herb gardens are used in the restaurant. ◈ *Midway between Safed and Rosh Pina • Map B5 • (04) 699 4555• www.mizpe-hayamim.com • $$$$$*

Genghis Khan in the Golan
Staying in Mongolian *yurts* (tents) in a *moshav* (cooperative settlement) in the Golan hills is an unusual experience. The large circular tents have mattresses on the floor, while shower rooms are outside. Kitchen facilities, and helpful hosts, are a plus. A dormitory tent is also available for those on a budget. ◈ *Givat Yoav, Lower Golan • Map C6 • 052 371 5687 • www. gkhan.co.il • $$$ Dorm $*

Fauzi Azar Inn
Down a Nazareth alleyway in a restored Arab mansion, this inn boasts characterful rooms and clean dorms. It is a great base for exploring Galilee. ◈ *Nazareth • Map C5 • (04) 602 0469 • www.fauzi azarinn.com • $$$ Dorm $*

Left **Yehelim** Right **Krivine's Guest House**

TOP 10 Lodgings in the Dead Sea & Negev

1 Krivine's Guest House

Located in Ovdat National Park, this quiet family-run guesthouse offers home-cooking and English-style hospitality. There is no TV, but they offer free Wi-Fi, laundry, and a communal space. Add spectacular desert vistas, hiking, biking, and herds of Ibex to the 320 days of sunshine. ◈ Neve Zin, Midrashet Sde Boker • Map A2 • (052) 271 2304 • www.krivines.com • $$

2 Khan Be'erotayim

This khan (inn) offers unique desert isolation near the ruins of Nitsana. Bare but spacious guestrooms are fashioned from date palms and mud, and share a delightfully rustic washroom. Camel treks and biking trails are followed by bonfires under starry skies. ◈ Near Ezuz, Nitsana • Map A2 • (08) 655 5788 • www.beerotayim.co.il • $$$–$$

3 Ein Gedi Country Hotel

Set within lush gardens, this hotel boasts awesome views of the Dead Sea and white cliffs. The rooms have quirky themes and good facilities. There is a seasonal pool, and use of the nearby spa and entrance to the Botanical Garden is included. ◈ Kibbutz Ein Gedi, the Dead Sea • Map G5 • (08) 659 4220/1 • www.ein-gedi.co.il • $$$$

4 IYHA Masada Guesthouse

This popular place with a prime location at the foot of Masada has well-equipped rooms with air-conditioning and TV, as well as dormitories. Book in advance. ◈ Masada • Map H5 • (02) 594 5622 • www.iyha.org.il • $$$ Dorms $

5 Yehelim

This boutique hotel boasts stunning desert views. The rooms are comfortable and the kosher home-cooked food is exceptional. Close to the western side of Masada, the area offers excellent hiking. ◈ 72 Moav St., Arad • Map H4 • (052) 652 2718 • www.yehelim.com • $$$$

6 Beresheet Hotel

Luxurious stone chalets, whose natural colors reflect the environment are offered here. Bathrooms are sumptuous, and many rooms have private pools. The bar almost hangs over the crater, and there's a spa. ◈ 1 Beresheet Rd., Mitspe Ramon • Map A2 • (08) 659 8004 • www.isrotel exclusivecollection.com • $$$$$

7 ibike

A cheerful guesthouse frequented by bikers and outdoor types. Rooms are unfussy, with contemporary styling. The hotel also has lovely communal spaces and a café. ◈ 4 Har Ardon, Spice Routes Quarter, Mitspe Ramon • Map A2 • (052) 4367878 • www.ibike.co.il • $$$

8 Green Backpackers

This little hostel has private rooms and spotless dorms. There is a cozy lounge, the kitchen is well equipped, and Wi-Fi is free. The crater of Makhtesh Ramon is close by. Ask the friendly owners for information on hiking. ◈ 10/6 Nahal Sirpad, Mitspe Ramon • Map A2 • (054) 690 7474 • www.thegreenback packers.com • $$ Dorms $

9 Herod's Palace

Guests are pampered at this imposing hotel, an Eilat landmark. The rooms aren't as wildly opulent as the public spaces, but the private beach and pool are excellent. There are also boutique and spa hotels in the complex, and many excellent restaurants and bars. ◈ North Beach, Eilat • Map C2 • (08) 638 0000 • www.herodshotels.com • $$$$$

10 Nova Like Hotel

Part of the Atlas chain, this good-value hotel has bold rooms with a bright, sunny feel. A reliable option, with decent standards and service for a reasonable price. ◈ 6 Hativat Hanegev St., Eilat • Map C2 • (08) 638 2444 • www.atlas.co.il • $$$–$$

There are many resort hotels in Ein Bokek and Eilat. Look online for good deals and packages.

Price Categories

For a standard, double room per night (with breakfast if included), taxes and extra charges.

$	under $50
$$	$50–110
$$$	$110–210
$$$$	$210–350
$$$$$	over $350

Above **Hilton Dahab Resort**

TOP10 Accommodations in Sinai & Petra

1 Four Seasons Hotel
Set amid lush gardens, this luxurious resort offers pools, a spa, and five innovative restaurants. Superb staff, but note that excursions are rather over-priced. *Sharm el-Sheikh • Map D2 • (069) 360.3555 • www. fourseasons.com • $$$$$*

2 Oonas Dive Club Hotel
A friendly hotel located on the more tranquil side of the bay. There's snorkeling off the beach, plus restaurants and bars nearby. Rooms are simple but include a fridge and TV. Catering primarily to divers, it's also the cheapest in Naama Bay. *Naama Bay, Sharm el-Sheikh • Map D2 • (069) 360 0581 • www.oonas diveclub.com • $*

3 Hilton Dahab Resort
Dahab's premier resort has pools, a private sandy beach, tastefully decorated Nubian-style rooms, and decent restaurants. It is a five-minute taxi ride from central Dahab. *Dahab City, Dahab • Map D2 • (069) 364 0310 • www.hilton.com • $$$–$$*

4 Nesima Resort
Located close to the sea and to Dahab's beach-cafés, the Nesima Resort has peaceful, landscaped grounds. The rooms are spotless and well-furnished, with domed ceilings. The restaurant is excellent and the staff is helpful. There is an on-site dive center. *Mashraba, Dahab • Map D2 • (069) 364 0320 • www.nesima-resort.com • $$*

5 Nakhil Inn & Nakhil Dream
Tarabin's upscale chalets have air-conditioning and TV, yet retain a rustic vibe. The soft sand beach has loungers and sunparasols, and offers opportunities for snorkeling, diving, and kayaking. It is a short stroll to beach cafés along the shore. *Tarabin, Nuweiba • Map C2 • (069) 350 0879 • www.nakhil-inn.com • $$*

6 Basata
An eco-camp located on the beach, Basata means "simplicity." You can camp, or choose from stylish chalets or cheerful huts. Evening meals are available, and there is also a kitchen for guests. *15 miles (24 km) north of Nuweiba • Map C2 • (069) 350 0480/1 • www.basata.com • $$ Camping $*

7 Monastery Guesthouse
Waking up in the Monastery grounds is a special feeling, next to the orchards and with Mount Sinai looming nearby. Rooms are comfortable but austere. Hearty meals are available, and the atmosphere is sociable. *St. Catherine's Monastery • Map D1 • (069) 347 0353, fax 347 0343 • $$*

8 Taba Heights Intercontinental Resort
The Intercontinental offers great value for a package holiday. The hotel boasts a spa and huge pools, while activities include golf, diving, and watersports. Restaurants, bars, and staff are all excellent. *Map C2 • (069) 358 0300 • www.ichotelsgroup.com • $$$–$$*

9 Möevenpick Resort Petra
The location of this resort, bang next to the Siq, is unbeatable. There's a pool and several restaurants, including a fabulous roof terrace – perfect for a drink after an exhausting day at the site. *Wadi Musa, Petra • Map B3 • +962 32157111 • www.moevenpick.com • $$$$*

10 Rocky Mountain Hotel
This is a sociable place to stay, enhanced by the extremely helpful management. It is modest but very clean, with free Wi-Fi and a good breakfast, plus amazing views from the terraces. A stiff climb from Petra, but free shuttles are available. *Main St., Wadi Musa • Map B3 • +962 3215 5100 • rockymountainhotel@yahoo.com • $*

General Index

Acknowledgements

Author A British travel writer and author, Vanessa Betts has spent more than a decade working overseas. She has lived in Israel, Egypt and India and authored several guidebooks covering these regions. She currently splits her time between Israel, Asia and the UK.

Photographer Idris Ahmed

Additional Photography Eddie Gerald; Rough Guides: Jean-Christophe Godet

Fact Checker Yaarah Chicorel

At DK INDIA

Managing Editor MadhuMadhavi Singh

Editorial Manager Sheeba Bhatnagar

Design Manager Mathew Kurien

Project Editor Vatsala Srivastava

Project Designer Aradhana Gupta

Assistant Cartographic Manager Suresh Kumar

Cartographer Schchida Nand Pradhan

Picture Research Manager Taiyaba Khatoon

Senior DTP Designer Azeem Siddiqui

Indexer Helen Peters

Proofreader Indira Chowfin

At DK LONDON

Publisher Vivien Antwi

List Manager Christine Stroyan

Senior Managing Art Editor Mabel Chan

Editorial Assistance Vicki Allen, Scarlett O'Hara, Debra Wolter

Designer Tracy Smith

Senior Cartographic Manager Casper Morris

Picture Research Assistant Marta Bescos Sanchez

Senior DTP Designer Jason Little

Production Controller Rita Sinha

Picture Credits

Placement Key: a-above; b-below/bottom; c-centre; f-far; l-left; r-right; t-top

Photography Permissions

Dorling Kindersley would like to thank the following for their assistance and kind permission to photograph at their establishments:

Abraham Hostel, Jerusalem; Al-Reda, Nazareth; Bible Lands Museum, Jerusalem; Bloomfield Science Museum, Jerusalem; Catit, Tel Aviv; Design Museum Holon; Eretz Israel Museum; Israel Children's Museum – Holon; Jerusalem Hotel; Krivine's Guest House; Lavan Restaurant, Jerusalem; Tel Aviv Museum of Art; Tikotin Museum of Japanese Art; Yad Vashem

The publisher would like to thank the following for their kind permission to reproduce their photographs:

ALAMY IMAGES: Stefano Baldini 4–5; dbimages 26–27c.

AMERICAN COLONY HOTEL: 112tr.

BROWN TLV URBAN HOTEL: 114tr.

CAMEL DIVE CLUB & HOTEL, SHARM EL-SHEIKH: 94tl.

THE CONTAINER: 74tl.

CORBIS: Nathan Benn 7cb, 24–25c; Mark Karrass 93cl; Richard T. Nowitz 25tc, 50clb; NSI Agency/Demotix 50tr; George Steinmetz 88–89; Roger Wood 27tl, 27bl.

EDDIE'S HIDEAWAY: 87tl.

FOUR SEASONS RESORT SHARM EL-SHEIKH, EGYPT: 95tl.

50tc; De Agostini 26cb; Borat Furlan 90cl; Hulton Archive/ Stringer 32tl; Popperfoto 32cra, 33tr; Jean Victor Schnetz 32tr.

HERBERT SAMUEL: 40tr; 75tl.

HILTON HOTELS & RESORTS: 117tl.

HOOHA CYCLING CLUB: 44t; 111tr.

HOTEL MONTEFIORE: 114tl.

IDRIS AHMED: 28cb; 28–29c; 29cb.

ISRAEL AIRPORTS AUTHORITY: 103tc.

ISRAEL MOUNTAIN GUIDES: 45cla.

ISRAEL MUSEUM JERUSALEM: 14cb; Simhat Torah flag, Jerusalem, 1950s, Print on cardboard, I : 34; W: 24.51 cm, Gift of Ayala Gordon, Jerusalem,/ Elie Posner 6cb; 1977–416, Mosaic floor, Church at Kissufim, 576–578, collection of The Israel Museum, Jerusalem/Vladimir Naikhin 14cla; Elie Posner 14–15c; Esther Scroll, Holland (?), 18th century, Pen and ink and gouache on parchment; handwritten, 25.5 x 297cm/Yoram Lehmann 15tl; Elie Posner 15cr; Reuven Rubin, Israeli, (b. Romania), 1893–1974, First Fruits, 1923, Oil on canvas, On loan from the Rubin Museum, Tel Aviv, H: 188; W: 102/Avi Hay 15clb; Reuven Rubin, Israeli, born Romania, 1893–1974, The Sea of Galilee, 1926–28, Oil on canvas, 65 x 81 cm, Anonymous gift to The Israel Museum, © Courtesy Rubin Museum, Tel Aviv/Peter Lanyi 16tl; The Rothschild Room - 18th-century French salon, 18th century, Gift of Baron Edmond and Baroness Nadine de Rothschild, Paris/David Harris 16tc; Amedeo Modigliani, Born Italy, active France, 1884–1920, Jeanne Hébuterne, Seated, 1918, Oil on canvas, 55 x 38 cm, Gift of Stella Fischbach, New York, to American Friends of the Israel Museum in memory of Harry Fischbach 16tr; Hanukkah lamp with a depiction of the prophet Zechariah's vision, Rome, Italy, 1810, Silver, cast, repoussé, engraved, and partly gilt, year 5570, H: 64; W: 44 cm, Gift of the Jewish Community of Rome/Elie Posner 17cl; The Tzedek ve-Shalom Synagogue, Paramaribo, Suriname, 1736/Elie Posner 17cr.

KIBBUTZ HOTELS CHAIN: 110tc.

MAMILLA HOTEL JERUSALEM: 60tr, 112tl.

MASTERFILE: Alberto Biscaro 22–23c, Robert Harding Images 27cr.

MINI ISRAEL: 37cla.

NESIMA RESORT: 94tr.

SHALVATA: 74tc.

TEL AVIV PERFORMING ARTS CENTER: 46cl.

YEHELIM BOUTIQUE HOTEL: 116tr.

All other images © Dorling Kindersley

For further information see: www. dkimages.com

Special Editions of DK Travel Guides

DK Travel Guides can be purchased in bulk quantities at discounted prices for use in promotions or as premiums. We are also able to offer special editions and personalized jackets, corporate imprints, and excerpts from all of our books, tailored specifically to meet your own needs.

To find out more, please contact:

(in the United States) **SpecialSales@dk.com**

(in the UK) **travelspecialsales@uk.dk.com**

(in Canada) DK Special Sales at **general@tourmaline.ca**

(in Australia) **business.development@pearson.com.au**

Phrase Book

Hebrew has an alphabet of 22 letters. As in Arabic, the vowels do not appear in the written language and there are several systems of transliteration. In this phrasebook we have given a simple phonetic transcription only. Bold type indicates the syllable on which the stress falls. An apostrophe between two letters means that there is a break in the pronunciation. The letters "kh" represent the sound "ch" as in Scottish "loch," and "g" is hard as in "gate." Where necessary, the masculine form is given first, followed by the feminine.

In Emergency

Help!	Hat**zi**lu!
Stop!	At**zor**!
Call a doctor!	**Az**minu ro**fe**!
Call an ambulance!	**Az**minu am**bu**lans!
Call the police!	Tzalt**ze**lu lamisht**a**ra!
Call the fire brigade!	Tzalt**ze**lu lemekha**bei** esh!
Where is the nearest telephone?	**E**fo hat**e**lefon hatzibu**ri** ha**khi** ka**rov**?
Where is the nearest hospital?	**E**fo bet hakho**lim** ha**khi** ka**rov**?

Communication Essentials

Yes	Ken
No	Lo
Please	Bevaka**sha**
Thank you	To**da**
Excuse me	Sli**kha**
Hello	Sha**lom**
Good day	**Bo**ker tov
Greetings (on the Sabbath)	Sha**bat** Sha**lom**
morning	**bo**ker
afternoon	a**khar** hatzoho**ryim**
evening	**e**rev
night	**lai**la
today	ha**yom**
tomorrow	ma**khar**
here	po
there	sham
what?	ma?
which?	**ei**zeh?
when?	ma**tai**?
who?	mi?
where?	**e**fo?

Useful Phrases

How are you?	Ma shlom**kha**/ shlo**mekh**?
Very well, thank you	Be**se**der, to**da**
Pleased to meet you	Na'im**me**od
Goodbye	Lehitra**ot**
(I'm) fine!	Be**se**der ga**mur**
Where is/Where are?	**E**fo…?
How many kilometres is it to…?	**Ka**ma kilo**me**trim mi**po** le…?
What is the way to…?	Ekh megi**im** le…?
Do you speak English?	**A**ta/at meda**ber**/ meda**be**ret ang**lit**?
I don't understand	A**ni** lo me**vin**/ mevi**na**

Useful Words

large	ga**dol**
small	ka**tan**
hot	kham
cold	kar
bad	lo tov
enough	mas**pik**
well	be**se**der
open	pa**tu**akh
closed	sa**gur**
left	smol
right	ya**min**
straight	ya**shar**
near	ka**rov**

far	ra**khok**
up	le**ma**la
down	le**ma**ta
soon	muk**dam**
late	meu**khar**
entrance	kni**sa**
exit	yet**zia**
toilet	sheru**tim**
free, unoccupied	pa**nui**
free, no charge	khi**nam**

Making a Telephone Call

I'd like to make a long-distance call	Ha**i**ti rot**ze**/rot**za** lehitka**sher** le**khutz** la**ir**
I'd like to make a reversed-charge call	Ha**i**ti rot**ze**/rot**za** lehitka**sher** gova**i**na
I'll call back later	Etka**sher** meu**khar** yo**ter**
Can I leave a message?	Ef**shar** lehash**ir** hoda'**a**?
Hold on	Ham**tin**/ham**ti**ni (Tam**tin**/tam**ti**ni)
Could you speak up a little, please?	Tu**khal**/tuk**hli** leda**ber** be**kol** ram yo**ter**?
local call	**si**kha iro**nit**
international call	**si**kha benleu**mit**

Shopping

How much does it cost?	**Ka**ma zeh o**leh**?
I would like…	Ha**i**ti rot**zeh**/rot**za**…
Do you have…?	Yesh la**khem**…?
I'm just looking.	A**ni** rak mista**kel**/ mista**ke**let.
Do you take credit cards?	A**tem** mekab**lim** karts**ei** ashr**ai**?
Do you take traveller's cheques?	A**tem** mekab**lim** traveller's cheques?
What time do you open?	Ma**tai** pot**khim**?
What time do you close?	Ma**tai** sog**rim**?
this one	zeh
that one	ha**hu**
expensive	Ya**kar**
inexpensive/cheap	lo ya**kar**/zol
size	mi**da**

Staying in a Hotel

I have a reservation	Yesh li azma**na**
Do you have a free room?	Yesh la**khem** **khe**der pa**nui**?
double room	**khe**der zu**gi**
room with two beds	**khe**der im sh**tei** mi**tot**
room with a bath or a shower	**khe**der im sheru**tim** ve amb**at**ia o ik**la**khat
single room	**khe**der ya**khid**
key	maf**te**akh
lift	ma'a**lit**

Eating Out

Have you got a table free?	Yesh la**khem** shul**khan** pa**nui**?
I would like to book a table	Ha**i**ti rot**ze**/rot**za** lehaz**min** shul**khan**
The bill please	Kheshb**on**, bevaka**sha**
I am vegetarian	A**ni** tzimkho**ni**/ tzimkho**nit**
menu	taf**rit**
fixed-price menu	taf**rit** is**kit**
wine list	taf**rit** hayei**not**
glass	kos
bottle	bak**buk**
knife	sa**kin**
spoon	kaf
fork	mas**leg**
breakfast	aru**khat** **bo**ker
lunch	aru**khat** tzoho**ryim**
dinner	aru**khat** **e**rev

Arabic Phrase Book

Transliteration from Arabic script to the Roman alphabet is a difficult task. Although many attempts have been made, there is no satisfactory system and you will repeatedly come across contradictory spellings in Egypt.

In this phrase book we have given a simple phonetic transcription only. The underlined letter indicates the stressed syllable.

Pronunciation

a,-ah	as in "mad"
aa	as in "far"
aw	as in "law"
ay	as in "day"
e	as in "bed"
ee	as in "keen"
i	as in "bit"
o	as in "rob"
oo	as in "food"
u	as in "book"
A	pronounced as an emphasised "a" as in "both of us – you And me!"
D	a heavily pronounced "d"
gh	like a French "r" – from the back of the throat
H	a heavily pronounced "h"
kh	as in the Scottish pronunciation of "loch"
q	a "k" sound from the back of the mouth as in "caramel"
S,T	heavily pronounced "s", "t"
th	as in "thin"
Z	heavily pronounced "z"
'	this sounds like a small catch in the breath

In Emergency

Help!	an-najdah!
Stop!	qeff!
I want to go to a doctor	oreed al zehab lel tabeeb
I want to go to a pharmacist	oreed al zehab lel saydaliya
Where is the nearest telephone?	ayn yoogad aqrab telifoon?
Where is the hospital?	ayn yoogad al mostashfa?
I'm allergic to... penicillin/aspirin	Andee Hasaaseeyah men penicillin/aspirin

Communication essentials

Yes/No	naAm/laa
Thank you	shokran
No, thank you	laa shokran
Please (asking for something)	min faDlak
Please (offering)	tafaDal
Good morning	sabaaH al-khayr
Good afternoon	as-salaam Alaykum
Good evening	masa' al-khayr
Good night	teSbaH Ala khayr (when going to bed)
Good night (leaving group early)	maA as-salaamah or as-salaam Alaykum
Goodbye	maA as-salaamah
Excuse me, please	min faDlak, law samaHt
today	al-yawm
yesterday	al-ams
tomorrow	ghadan
here	hona
there	honaak
what?	maza?
which?	ay?
when?	mata?
who?	man?
where?	ayn?

Useful Phrases

I don't understand	la afham
Do you speak English	hal tatakalam engleezee/
I can't speak Arabic	la ataklam al Arabeya
I don't know	la aAref
My name is...	esmee...
How are you?	kayf Haalak?
Sorry!	aasef
Can you tell me...?	men fadlak qol lee...?
I would like....?	oreed...
Is there...here?	yugad...hona?
Where can I get...?	ayn ajed...?
How much is it?	kam thaman haza (m) hazeehee (f)?
Do you take credit cards?	hal taqbal Visa, Access?
Where is the toilet?	ayn ajed al-hamam?
left	yasaar
right	yameen
up	fawq
down	asfal

Travel

I want to go to...	oreed al zehab le...
How do you get to...	kayef tazhab le...?
I'd like to rent a car	oreed asta'jer sayaarah
driver's licence	rokhSat qiyaadah
petrol/gas	banzeen
petrol/gas station	maHaTTat banzeen
When is there a flight to...?	mata toogad reHalat tayaran ela...?
What is the fare to...?	kam thaman al tazkarah le...?
A ticket to...please	law samaHt, tazkarat zehaab le...

Making a Telephone Call

may I use your telephone?	momken astaAmel teleefoonak
How much is a call to...?	be-kam al-mokaalamah le...?
Can I call abroad from here?	momken ataSel bel-khaarej men hona?
My number is...	raqamee...
telephone call	mokaalamah
emergency	Tawaare'
operator	sentraal

Staying in a Hotel

Have you got any vacancies?	hal yoogad ghoraf khaaleeyah?
I have a reservation	Andee Hajz
I'd like a room with a bathroom	oreed ghorfah be-Hammam
May I have the bill please?	momken al-hesab law samaHat
I'll pay by credit card	sa-asfaA al-fatoorah law Visa, Access
I'll pay by cash	sa-adfaA naqdan
hotel	fondoq
air-conditioning	takyeef
double room	ghorfa mozdawajah
single room	ghorfa be-sareer waaHed
shower	dosh
toilet	towaaleet
toilet paper	waraq towaleet
key	meftaaH
lift/elevator	mesAd
breakfast	foToor
restaurant	maTAm
bill	faatoorah

Town and Street Index